The Insider's Guide to
Household
Staffing 2ᴺᴰ ED.

Private Staffing Secrets
They DO Want You to Know!

David Gonzalez

ISBN: 1496153774
ISBN-13: 9781496153777

Table of Contents

Preface vii

Introduction ix

How to use this book. xi

Private Service Professionals 1

Private Service Associations. 2

Professional's View: Ted Hadley. 5

Private Service Roles and Titles 9

Household Staff - Job Descriptions and Functions 11

Estate Manager. 11

Private Service Profile: Gary Warstler. 15

Butler / House Manager 19

Expert's View: Charles MacPherson 22

Private Service Profile: Robert Hayman 24

Personal Assistant. 26

Expert's View - Bonnie Low-Kramen. 29

Personal / Private Chef or Household Cook 36

Private Service Profile: Mike Neylan 39

Domestic Couple 41

Support Staff. 43

Private Service Profile: Elizabeth Stone,
Executive Housekeeper. 45

Additional Private Service Profiles: Julie Mills, Personal Assistant. 49

Additional Private Service Profiles: Onna Lil Salerno, Executive Housekeeper. 52

Additional Private Service Profiles: Estella Ferrer, House Manager 54

Additional Private Service Profiles: Sean Sunkel, Estate Manager. 56

Private Service Employment. 61

Finding a Private Service Position. 61

Expert's View: Carol Scudere, Founder/Owner/Director, Professional Domestic Services and Institute 68

Becoming a Better Employment Candidate. 74

Job Seeker Basics. 76

Expert's View: Donna Shannon, Personal Touch Career Services 77

Interviewing: Remember the Premise 86

Principals with Principles – Job Search Standards and Errors . . 91

Writing, Language, and Terminology. 92

Telephone. 94

Email 99

Technology and Social Media 101

Working With Domestic Employment Agencies. 109

Discrimination?!? Yes. 114

Job Seeker's View: Alan Bussey 116

Expert's View: Feigon Hamilton 117

Private Service Employers 133

    Privacy? Please 133

    Expert's View: Glenn Greenhouse, Greenhouse Agency, Ltd. . . 134

    Client Self-Sabotage 136

    Your Own Worst Enemy – Do You Even Care? 140

    Expert's View: Julie Kroubetz 140

    Hiring Private Service Staff 144

    The Hiring Procedure (Do-It-Yourself / No Agency) 144

    Finding Staff through an Agency 152

    Interviewing Candidates 158

    Reference and Background Checks 163

    Checking References 163

    Background Checks 166

    Is There Something More....? 168

Conclusion 171

About the Author 175

Preface
About the Second Edition

Has it really been ten years? It's almost unimaginable that The Insider's Guide to Household Staffing was first published in 2002. At that time we were relatively new in the private staffing field and wrote this guide mainly to sort out the diverse information circulating through the agency side of the business. Standards and definitions were daily questions, along with policies and procedures for staffing and working in the estate environment. Our first version of the guide was a solid review of the agency's basics, current market and employment trends, and simple but practical advice for all parties in the hiring process. The book was very well received and has been in circulation over the years with great feedback from the private service audience. It remains an essential tool for anyone working as, employing, or recruiting a private service professional. Interestingly, though we are now ten years down the road, changes in the global economy that chart like a roller coaster have brought us back in range of the 2002 figures for compensation in our field. Those comparing numbers in both editions will see that the old figures still hold up well for estimating compensation for today's household positions. There will be a number of adjustments to the original content, but they won't be far off from the first version. The biggest changes, and the main reason to dig into the new edition will be found in the extensive additions, all-new advice, and detailed "secrets" that everyone needs to know. Secrets you say? Yes, secrets. We're revealing the unspoken, "behind the scenes", sometimes politically incorrect, real issues that factor into our process every day. Much of this information is not kept from the public because of confidentiality, but because of time and individual "need to know" circumstances. We unfortunately can't discuss every detail with every client and candidate we speak to, so we're writing it down. Our aim is to make this important knowledge base available to everyone, and the new book version you are about to explore offers just that.

Apart from the economic changes over the last ten years, we have seen enormous leaps in technology, communications, and protocols in the staffing arena. So many are being left behind by the onslaught of email, texting, file sharing, cloud computing, video interviews, online job boards, smart phones, smart homes, and more! We don't profess to be experts in every detail, but we are privy to thousands of interactions and scenarios every year involving the household employment process. We are simply reporting back to you where we've seen so many fail or succeed when it comes to misunderstood standards and protocols, new or old. In addition, understanding the perspectives, challenges, and concerns of others in private employment remains paramount. For this reason we've expanded significantly on the "what's really going on" tone and insight relative to today's private service marketplace. Many of the items presented for both employees and employers may seem a bit picky, harsh, or perhaps even controversial, but please keep in mind the end goal of sharing these insights: We are trying to improve understanding to create successful long term service relationships. And rest assured it won't just be our opinion. Throughout the book you'll hear from other experts in the field and glean tips from some of the most seasoned, "best in the business" contributors who have graciously added their expertise to our book. Without question there is something for everyone in the following pages. Enjoy!

Introduction
What is the purpose of this book?

This book was written based on the daily operation and concerns of a Domestic Employment Agency. It was my intention to elaborate on the information we give to clients and candidates each day while trying to create successful employment situations. Our business in its simplest form is managing an exchange of information, and the proper gathering and sharing of that information is what makes a good placement. This book should be used as a general guide by anyone involved in the private service employment process, whether as employee, employer, or agent. Some of the information will be relevant to your situation, and some will not. However, with a more complete understanding of each party's concerns, wants, needs, and challenges, it will be easier to see from the other's perspective and work toward a win-win relationship from the very start. For many of the topics in the guide there are not 100% correct answers, and it will be easy to find several points of view on a number of items. Our goal is to present a well-rounded compilation of the most common and widely accepted terms and standards as they apply to private service today. The information comes from a number of sources including long-time domestic staff, professional staffing agencies, clients, and my own experience interacting with the households of "Ultra high net worth" (UHNW) families around the world. No matter what your purpose is for reading this book, you should be able to take away some useful knowledge that will apply to your future success in a private service career, as an employer of household staff, or as a placement agent.

Another very important, if not the most important, reason for this book is to help educate all parties in the private service relationship about the expectations we have for each other. The greatest failures we see over time in private staffing are a direct result of unstated, or ambiguous expectations by any one side of the relationship. When employers cannot or do not articulate clearly what they expect for their service standards, the employee will either be lost in a guessing game or simply fall short of what the employer had in their mind alone. Similarly, if a service provider has needs and expected results in their role that are never communicated, they tend to end up resentful and feeling unappreciated, or simply confused about how to engage their employer over the long term. The same goes for the agency role. This guide has much to offer in dealing with the agency functions and relationship for both employers and job seekers. In fact, it may be even more essential to communicate well when using an agency so they can effectively transfer information as the "middle man," properly representing the two sides of the relationship.

Overall, communication is the key element - not just in what we communicate, but also how we go about it. Never underestimate the power of an idea that is clearly spoken and delivered kindly! There must be respectful and healthy dialogue to work through the hiring and employment process together. In fact, one thing that will always be a "black and white" issue for us is that we will never work with anyone who is intentionally mean, vindictive, or abusive within the service relationship. There is just no room to accommodate that behavior in service. We all have needs, but we never need to accept abusive behavior from anyone in the service flow, as either an employer or a service provider. We've eliminated a number of candidates and "fired" a handful of clients from our agency for this exact reason, and encourage others to respectfully ask for civil, professional behavior from all involved in service employment.

We hope to continue to serve the industry with open dialogue, educational opportunities and materials, and most of all with an uncompromising business ethic. All of our information is intended to continually discover and present the highest standards in private service, which many consider to be the epitome of service excellence. We hold ourselves to that measure and strive to learn more along the way, helping others in their pursuit of exceptional service relationships.

How to use this book

It is certainly recommended that you read the whole guide straight through, but when returning to reference certain sections or focus on a specific topic, the contents outline will offer quick access. We encourage each reader to consider the sections and perspectives of both the employer and service staff. There are so many hints and tidbits of information to be picked up when approaching the relationship from each angle, that you will undoubtedly find it worthwhile to examine every facet. Enjoy!

Private Service Professionals

Over the last decade in the Household Staffing marketplace there have been occasional attempts to standardize terms and definitions for the profession. There are several names and descriptions that have been, and remain, timeless. However, the business as a whole has struggled to find consistent standards and to be recognized in a professional light. To combat this a number of industry veterans and domestic agency participants have organized groups or associations where these items could be sorted out to some degree. Additionally, in the daily course of business, agencies, clients, and job applicants discuss the titles, duties, and standards for each position relative to the client's home. Here there arises a "common ground" for understanding the terms everyone agrees to use and helps identify roles within the field in a more flexible, ongoing way. Lastly, the several schools in private service throughout the world have their standard definitions to look to as a reference both historically and for the modern era.

Private Service Staff have many titles, roles, and functions within the employer's home. They include every task from washing dishes to coordinating the purchase, remodel, and decoration of multiple, international properties. In larger homes (approx. 15k sq. ft. plus) there usually exists a greater need for structured management in addition to the service personnel. These are situations where owners are no longer capable of overseeing the staff or simply have chosen to pay someone else to take on the responsibility. It is at the management or expert level where lengthy experience is invaluable, and proper staffing can determine the overall comfort level of the owners.

In this guide we are concerned with the home that requires a more structured staff. Though there are many positions holding equal importance within a home, our focus is on the management and skilled professional service jobs. These include:

Estate Managers

Butlers

House Managers

Personal Assistants

Private Chefs

Domestic Couples

Other titles and positions will be briefly covered as "support staff." Though not the main focus of the guide, all of the advice presented for employers and employees will apply equally to any private service job.

Private Service Associations

With the main goals being unity and recognition within the industry over the last ten years, three distinct groups launched efforts to unite private service providers, domestic agencies, and related vendors. The earliest was established and promoted by the Starkey International Institute for Household Management. Their school held annual conferences called *Restoring the Art* and gathered industry professionals from across the country, with some coming from outside the USA as well. A formal association was built during these gatherings called the International Association of Service Professionals (IASP). We were charter members of the group and it lasted only about a year due to the complexities and requirements for such an association to obtain status as a non-profit. Not much happened beyond the official formation of the group. It seemed to be a step in the right direction, but the all-volunteer organization never gained enough momentum to continue with its original plans.

Second, once again springing from the efforts of those gathered at the Starkey events, a newer version of the same idea came to life. The similarly named International Association For Private Service Professionals (IAPSP) began with a solid backing of service providers, agencies, and the Starkey School. Like the organization before it, this association would be all volunteer and had goals to provide standards in the industry, gain tax-exempt status, and even run a proper apprentice program that met government qualifications. The initial success of the new group was very welcomed in the business. Within a year and a half the IAPSP organized and held a national conference similar to the Starkey events of the past. There was a very good crowd for an inaugural event and things were looking good for the IAPSP to continue. Unfortunately the economic times took a bad turn in 2008, and money was tight for many in the service profession. Talk of a second annual event faded away as the time for planning passed by. There seemed less and less interest in joining a group with annual dues and traveling to an event for continuing education and networking. The focus for most was on maintaining their position with an employer or finding any decent work within the field at all. Little more was heard about future plans of the group.

Subsequently, as the IAPSP seemed to fade in its efforts and reach, a new group emerged from the Midwest with a slightly different approach. With a strong focus on the vendors who cater to high net worth households, the Domestic Estate Manager's Association (DEMA) started to gather steam. The group chose to organize without a tax exemption and emphasized the relationship between vendors selected for hire in private homes and the Household Managers who often handle the vendor relationships. The organization developed a strong online presence and focused efforts on building local chapters throughout the USA. With a number of successful chapters up and running, DEMA held its inaugural national conference in September of 2012 in Los Angeles. We were fortunate enough to participate as a sponsor and panelist at one of the general sessions, and can say that the event was very well done on many levels. A second event is scheduled for late 2013 and there seems to be a high level of interest among past and new participants. Time will tell if this organization's shifted focus will yield continued growth and long term results as an international association.

In addition to the groups mentioned here, there are other bodies organizing for the support of domestic workers. Their main goals seem to be fair treatment and employment laws covering domestic staff. To discuss the legal and ethical implications of employing staff would be far beyond the scope of this book, and more appropriately handled through a referral to experts in the field. We are also assuming the readers of our book will seek to employ staff fairly and consult with the corresponding advisor on how to do so for their particular situation.

Overall, we are pleased to see and support efforts in the private service industry to organize and raise professional standards. We hope the interest and momentum continues for any group that is lifting up the profession and improving service relationships.

Professional's View: Ted Hadley

Ted Hadley is a Private Service Professional who was looking for a position in early 2013. He is registered with our agency and we met personally at the DEMA conference in September 2012. I invited Ted to write a short piece about his background in private service, some ideas on important skills, and his impression of the industry.

"I have extensive experience running homes and businesses, most recently in Princeville on the island of Kaua'i (the "Garden Isle" of Hawai'i). For the past six years, I have provided a wide range of services for home and vacation rental owners of this world-class destination. My discerning clients expect only the best, and I constantly strive to deliver the highest levels of professional service. Services have included staging and unstaging properties for clients' personal use, cleaning and preparation for vacation rental use, periodic deep cleaning, general maintenance and repairs, troubleshooting, contractor management, concierge-type services to guests, being the "eyes & ears" for off-island principals, and being on call 24/7 as a first responder for emergencies.

Prior to moving to Kaua'i, I've spent most of my adult life in the greater San Francisco Bay Area. I have over 10 years' experience in the real-time software, telecommunications, and health care industries in Silicon Valley and the Monterey Bay Area. Some of the key transferable skills I bring from my business experience to my domestic service include:

-A Master's Certificate in Project Management from AT&T.
-Years of Documentation and Training experience.
-Microsoft Certified Professional - Microsoft Office Master.

-A wide variety of experience managing both in-house and contractor staff.

-And a broad array of Scheduling, Financial & Budgeting skills.

My academic career includes over three years in Europe, culminating in a Master's Degree in French Civilization from the Sorbonne in Paris. I am fluent in English, French, German, and Spanish. I've also studied Culinary Arts and enjoy preparing and serving fine food and wine, formal entertaining, and travel.

My career transition to domestic service has been a gradual one, at first just helping to fill in for my wife's home services company occasionally when she needed extra handyman or cleaning help. After owning our own homes and raising a son, I had plenty of practical experience with sweat equity home improvement projects-- no job too big or too small. Over time, the majority of my time was spent this way, helping to serve multiple clients in parallel. Recently, we decided it would make more sense for us if I were to make this my full-time career dedicated to serving just one family.

To that end, I began applying my previous quality management experience into researching the emerging industry of domestic service. I was on the lookout for key players, standards, and ways to both fit in and stand out as a professional. As a result of that research, I became a member of the *Domestic Estate Managers Association* (DEMA) and attended the first national convention in 2012 in Los Angeles. I am also currently enrolled with the *International Institute of Modern Butlers* (IIMB) pursuing a Certificate in Butler/Estate management.

At the DEMA national convention, I was able to meet the chairman and founder of the IIMB, Mr. Steven Ferry, personally. I also attended many valuable seminars, including *30 Productivity Tips Using Windows 7 & Office 2010* by Vickie Evans of RedCape Company, a frequent co-presenter with Bonnie Low-Kramen, Instructor/Author of *Be the Ultimate Assistant*, one of the most widely recognized leaders in our emerging industry. I mention these events as samples among many because I think they speak to the evolving nature of the domestic service industry and its coming of age. In my opinion and past experience in other industries, a key aspect to being a professional is the recognition and adherence to standards.

After the convention I followed up on one of Ms. Evans' tips and took the necessary steps to prepare for and pass the exams to become a Microsoft Certified Professional - Microsoft Office Master. This is one way I felt I could differentiate myself as a professional, with independent confirmation of a skill set that's widely recognized and used on a regular basis.

There's an expression: *The One Constant Is Change*. One part of being a professional is staying current with the ever-changing needs of our employers. One of the most important skills to be successful in domestic service is to be able to listen and communicate effectively with many different kinds of people. Serving as liaison between principals and staff requires constant awareness of changing needs among all parties. Finding ways to find the best answers, as measured by commonly recognized industry standards through a network of professionals, is a key milestone in our industry's evolution."

We encourage everyone's involvement with networking and training through any reputable organization. Professional development is paramount in any industry and private service is no exception. Learning from others and continuing to recognize the field as a respected profession will produce immediate and future benefits for all.

Private Service Roles and Titles

One of the items that has seemed to stick via the efforts of the service associations is this chapter's title, "Private Service Professionals." The term was developed, adopted, and carried through the industry as we have all tried to move away from the general terms of "servant" or "domestic." Though still widely in use, the older, more broad terms needed a better defined idea for those who make a career in private service, especially in the high net worth environment, and certainly at a managerial level. This new term will likely apply to those with a lengthy career history in private service, a formal education within the field, clearly defined management status in the home, or a combination of the above.

The following section offers a look at the various roles of Private Service Professionals. Since it is written from the agency perspective, we focus on the main positions and titles common to our clients' requests. Throughout the world there will be different specific meanings associated with each title, but the general categories and skills seem to be consistent with what we present here. Again, this information has been compiled over many years of learning and interacting with clients, service personnel, and institutions for service education. We welcome any correction, addition, or comment on the information we provide, as it seems the profession is still fluid and constantly reinventing itself with the times, remaining open to discussion on the finer points.

Author's Note: When we discuss titles with clients we often suggest that they can call a position whatever they want. Though true, different titles will offer either more clarity to a particular role or present a certain image that the employee can adopt. We also can use a "working title" for better describing the position to potential candidates as we conduct a search for the right fit. There are countless combinations and it is up to all parties to determine which makes the most sense for communicating the proper context of the job.

Household Staff - Job Descriptions and Functions

Estate Manager

Title

Estate Manager is perhaps the most widely used term in the business. Most candidates with a bit of experience running a household will mistakenly call themselves an Estate Manager. Likewise, other terms can be confused with it such as Majordomo, House Manager, and Butler. However, it is important to recognize the overall scope of the Estate Manager, being held in high regard as the top position title in private service. Some other variations may include "Director of Estates," "Director of Properties," and "Chief of Staff," but with a clear picture of the Estate Manager's functions and a working definition of "Estate," it is easy to see who truly fits the position. A common abbreviation for those in the industry is "EM."

Author's Note: One of the greatest pleasures of my career as a private service agency owner has been learning from the vast array of employees we get to know over time. It has always amazed me to meet and speak with Estate Managers who are deep in their years of service to elaborate estates and intriguing clients. The many skills and experiences make for what some would call a modern day version of the "Renaissance Man." I continue to learn as we hear from these great service professionals in a field that is unique and rarely understood due to the privacy and discretion we all must honor.

Environment

The first qualifier we must consider is, "what defines as an estate?" Pulling from the online dictionaries [dictionary.com] we find several meanings:

noun

1. a piece of landed property, especially one of large extent with an elaborate house on it: to have an estate in the country.
2. Law.
a. property or possessions.
b. the legal position or status of an owner, considered with respect to property owned in land or other things.
c. the degree or quantity of interest that a person has in land with respect to the nature of the right, its duration, or its relation to the rights of others.
d. interest, ownership, or property in land or other things.
e. the property of a deceased person, a bankrupt, etc., viewed as an aggregate. Under the meanings associated with an elaborate home and grounds and/or the sum total of properties and possessions owned, we place the Estate Manager as the highest appointed role within a client's private staff.

Geographically, the Estate Manager would be located near the primary residence or offices of the Principal and have a "home office" of their own to base their administrative activity. When multiple properties are held, the EM is usually a travel based role with oversight duties at the various locations. In this instance the EM will go mobile with their operations, employing the latest technology and communications to run things from their fingertips while on the road.

Functions

Estate Manager is the top level in the household. He or she works directly with the owners to plan and execute the overall management of property and service. Where there are large or multiple homes the Estate Manager is the "C.E.O." of the organization, carrying out the wishes of the owner at each location. Estate Managers typically set the service standard and are responsible for the hiring, training, and ongoing management of staff required to meet the service needs of the household. In addition to personnel management, the administrative functions are many. All related financial matters including accounting, budgets, and payroll normally pass through the EM's hands. Based on the size of the property the Estate Manager may wear many other hats or delegate these functional areas to dedicated experts in the employer's stable. Interfacing with accountants, attorneys, curators, captains, pilots, architects, financial advisors, and more is par for the course. Common direct supervision tasks may include screening and overseeing outside vendors, contractors, construction projects, maintenance of grounds, collections, autos, yachts, private planes, etc. With multiple properties, most EM's travel ahead of their employer to get a property ready for their arrival and bring the staff up to speed on any necessary changes or service requirements. An Estate Manager may also be called upon to plan and execute events for the owner. This could range from a simple dinner for eight to a grand, formal gathering for eight hundred. For this mode an EM would regularly connect with top caterers, event planners, temporary service staff, and entertainment agencies. The levels of "hands-on" involvement can vary, but to truly exemplify the Estate Manager title, the details of service are executed primarily via management, and not as a service provider.

Qualification

The top Estate Managers in the industry are some of the most well rounded workers that can be found anywhere. The unique combination required to succeed in this position is rarely found in other professions. Important abilities include:

-Highest level of personal service experience with private families and/or individuals.
-Well educated in luxury items such as fine art and antiques.
-Proper social etiquette and cultural knowledge.
-Acute business skills in areas of finance, computers, planning, and organization.
-Human resources management.
-Leadership and motivation skills.
-Independent and team project management.
-Creative and intuitive thinking and problem solving.
-Very resourceful.
-Extremely well-traveled.
-Up to date on applicable technologies and global communications.
-Negotiating skills.
-Often multi-lingual.
-College or other advanced degree.
-Service training for private and/or hotel environments.

Above all, the right person for the job will be adaptable to the standards and desires of the employer. Execution of plans and tasks can be taught and developed with a basic skill set, but only those who are truly "in sync" with their boss and environment will succeed for the long term.

One variation worth mentioning is the substitution of a Family Office for the estate management function. We have worked with a few management companies who handle the Estate Manager's duties as a group. They involve several specialists to coordinate and maintain the vast holdings of the employers and sometimes include extended family's properties. For example, they may have a specialized real estate department to oversee acquisitions, renovations, and sales of global properties. A second specialist may work with staffing and training for the service needs throughout the homes, and another might be an inventory and insurance expert for all collections held. There are many potential configurations on the larger, global scale, but in our niche we will be referring to the individual who heads the overall estate regardless of any additional supporting personnel or office.

Compensation
The typical salary range is $100,000 - $200,000, while some Estate Managers in service for many years or with specialized project skills can earn in the range of $250,000 and up. Additional benefits may include fully paid housing, automobile, insurance, paid travel, clothing allowance, and more. One of the main factors for earning at the top of the range is the level of financial accountability this role has. Is there critical decision making at the purchasing, planning, construction, or other business transaction that would cause a profit or loss under the EM's direction? If so, the real value presented to an employer can be easily measured. We've seen bonuses given for project completion or meeting budget goals, and some salaries or bonuses have been tied directly to the employer's own financial success. When the scope of the job affects the bottom line, the compensation has the potential to continue upwards. Many in the high net worth category employ a "pay for performance" model, not uncommon in the financial industries where many of our clients derive their wealth.

Private Service Profile: Gary Warstler

Gary is an Estate Manager with a wide ranging service background and formal Chef training. We asked him to describe some of the highlights of his private service career that has spanned many years and roles, from a dedicated Private Chef to a top level Estate Manager covering eight properties and multiple staff for a high net worth employer.

Job Duties and Responsibilities:

"As an Estate Manager, I am responsible for managing all aspects of a large home or multiple properties. My duties include: facility care, observation and repair; budget, verifying and payment of all household finances; entertaining, event planning, execution and cleanup; staff management, payroll, scheduling, service standards, and team development. Special duties may include wardrobe care (couture); fine art: registration, shipping, receiving and installation; wine cellar management (valuation, storing, drinkability and food pairing); pet care; elder care; vehicle care; coordination with all other service staff team members for all additional needs; and providing convenience, care and comfort for the principals.

The root of good stewardship can usually be reduced to the critical everyday items: Do the lights come on? Is the temperature good? Do the TV, computer and telephone work?"

How did I get started in my career?

"After 25 years in the restaurant and catering business I was looking for a career change. A colleague suggested domestic staffing and referred me to an agent. After meeting with a couple of agents I learned that although my background and disposition would be a great fit for domestic staffing, I needed credentials and experience in Private Service. Upon graduating from The International Butler Academy I was able to get some temporary work through my network of agents. Within months I was very fortunate to have been offered my first full time, permanent position as an Estate Manager of eight properties."

What I enjoy most about my job:
"I very much enjoy the service side of this business. I love the feeling of taking care of a home and creating a comfortable environment for my employers and fellow staff members. I enjoy the challenge of anticipating the needs of my employers, being one step ahead so that everything has been taken care of before they need it. I enjoy the project management side of the business. I enjoy being involved in every aspect of a project from beginning to end and the sense of accomplishment when a project is completed to my employer's satisfaction. I also enjoy the financial benefits of this business – In exchange for tireless dedication, employment packages typically include a decent salary, accommodations, health and retirement plans."

What it takes to be successful:
"Project management skills – know the scope of work, budgets, resources, and timelines, executing efficiently.

Knowledge of how to care for luxury items – couture, fine linens, art, wine, cars, boats, private jets and familiarity with the latest home technology.

Ability to Network – ability to develop a network of high end service providers (experts in high end upholstery, carpet cleaning, dry cleaning, home repairs).

Solid Interpersonal skills - have the demeanor and willingness to work with a variety of personalities, life events and experiences within the household.

Strong communication skills – discover the communication style of the principal, what works best for them and frequency- How involved do they want to be? How often? (Minute by minute? Once the project/issue has been resolved?). How do they want to be reached? (Texts, emails, phone calls, face to face updates?). Be proactive!

Flexibility- The ability to be flexible with your time, and being able to change course in short notice.

Positive collaborative attitude - Willing to do whatever is required to get the work done. This often means helping with housekeeping, laundry, and other duties that are outside of your day to day responsibilities."

One of my favorite stories from the job:
"I once traveled with a family as their private chef for a holiday in Provence. It was 'living the dream' for a Parisian trained American chef to be able to cook all the flavors of summer. As a precise planner, the challenge was to stay flexible and see what the market provided once on location. I packed a couple of knives and waited to see what I might find. I found a fully stocked kitchen of small wares and a $30,000 stove. EUREKA!!! The open market was so abundant I was delirious. Too many choices, too little time. My French co-workers kept saying, 'This is Provence, Gary, be tranquil, stay cool.' For ten days following a day of sightseeing and excursion, I would return to the kitchen and cook. For ten evenings we sat on the outdoor terrace, looking over the infinity pool toward the village in the valley and watched the colors and hues of a southern France sunset and dusk while feasting on some awesome, multi-course meals. It was delicious and so very memorable. Every summer since, the family still marks the occasion with a note of remembrance."

Butler / House Manager

Title

The titles of Butler and House Manager (HM) are often inter-changeable and can have the most varied meanings in the busi-ness. Interpretation is usually a result of the employer's other staff and management structure, as well as their cultural background. Regardless of which title is chosen, the expected functions and abili-ties can be very similar. In a more complex, single residence, the Butler or HM may be strictly administrative in their duties, like a lo-calized version of the Estate Manager. For instance, a 30,000 square foot home's service and maintenance needs rival a small hotel, and just the office based coordination of all elements fills a full time, high level job. We might then see a variation on the title to include Butler Administrator, or Administrative Household Manager.

Environment

Butlers and House Managers can be found in homes of all sizes de-pending on the service needs of the owners. A House Manager is more likely to be in charge of a single residential property and have a closer relationship to the personal services in a smaller home. It is not uncommon these days to see an HM employed by a busy family in a house under 5000 square feet in order to meet a high service ex-pectation and relieve the owners of running the home. A Butler/HM that provides high levels of personal service might even live within the home or on the employer's property.

Functions

The International Guild of Professional Butlers describes the duties of a Butler as follows:

"A Butler typically: Oversees the household staff usually of one resi-dence. Understands concepts like being anticipatory, friendly not familiar, privacy and confidentiality, invisible and available. Answers residence phone, receives guests at the door and supervises the reception of visitors. Assists with staff training and organizes the duties and schedule of domestic staff. May assist or be charged with keeping the household budgets and inventory supplies. May schedule and oversee vendors of contracted services. May assist with household and family security measures. Oversees family packing and travel preparations. Understands social etiquette and formal service. Assists with planning and organizing parties and events in the home. Oversees and participates in proper table settings and entertainment prep. Serves meals and drinks and performs wait services related thereto. Knowledgeable about wines and spirits and oversees the wine cellar and liqueur inventory. May also serve as personal valet to the household and/or gentleman of the house. Performs light housekeeping duties. Coordinates with other staff as needed as well as with other parts of the employer's organization." [The International Guild of Professional Butlers Website, 2001] Other functions and skills may include:

-Cleaning and maintenance
-Care of clothing.
-Care of fine china, silver, crystal.
-Care and inventory of artwork and antiques.
-Maintenance of automobiles.
-Security of their employer and residence.
-Co-ordination and scheduling of service contractors.

As you can see, the all-around skills required of the Butler or House Manager are very similar to the Estate Manager. One main difference, however, is the level of "hands-on" involvement that is commonly present in the role. In the Butler/HM position, one may perform the service tasks themselves in addition to delegating to other staff. An HM or Butler can usually be relied upon to fill in for sick or absent staff at a moment's notice, or regularly support various other full time employees with their daily functions. For example, a

House Manager may assist with clothing care or a Butler with laundry or formal table service (This is often part of the Butler role). In residences with both an Estate Manager and HM/Butler, the two will work like a President and Vice President, administrating to the rest of the staff. It has recently become common for a House Manager to cook family style meals on a regular basis in smaller homes that require less overall care and can't justify a full-time chef.

It is also worth noting that in some households the title of Butler still has a certain old world connotation. The very formal service standards of a Royal Palace or traditional British culture are upheld in some US homes today. In these instances, again, the final job description rests within the wishes of the one being served, and the all-around skills of the employee should be compatible with the expected demands of the employer.

Qualification
Similar to the Estate Manager, the House Manager has a very broad range of skills and knowledge. Backgrounds range from Hotel and Restaurant Management to formal Butler school training. Others simply "fall" into the field by helping out a friend of the family at their home or crossing over from an assistant or nanny position. Many homes require only part-time help to ease the burden of the owners' busy schedules, but most families quickly realize the value of having a full-time person. Like all positions, the family's service needs and property size will dictate the duties and level of formality for the Butler/House Manager. Useful traits include:

-Office or restaurant management and service skills. (More formal background or schooling depending on the household.)
-Broad knowledge of household items and their care.
-Good social skills and personnel management.
-Business and technology capability including computers and accounting.

-Leadership and motivation skills.

-Independent and team project management.

-Problem solving and "get it done" attitude. Very "hands-on" and ready to pitch in.

-Very resourceful, quickly learns the how and where to get things done in the local area.

-Negotiating and supervisory skills for outside contractors and other staff.

Again, the right person for the job will be adaptable to the standards and desires of the employer. Less formal households may choose to hire someone with related skills simply because they like their personality and can be trusted, while a more formal, larger organization will tend toward an extremely seasoned and perhaps formally schooled candidate. The Estate Manager or the owners themselves will sometimes be able to train the Butler / House Manager on the necessary and specific procedures of the home. In most cases, however, a well trained Butler with years of experience in similar households is the only consideration.

Compensation
Typical salary range is $70,000 - $120,000. More formal or specialized service requirements, a higher number of employees supervised, more demanding family and entertainment schedules, and related complexities will dictate higher pay rates. Additional benefits may include fully paid housing, automobile, insurance, clothing allowance, and more.

Expert's View: Charles MacPherson
The following excerpt is from the new book *The Butler Speaks*, by Charles MacPherson, Founder of The Charles MacPherson Academy for Butlers and Household Managers.

What is a Butler?...I believe a good Butler should exhibit the following characteristics:

-A desire to serve
-Discretion
-Interest
-Ability to anticipate
-Curiosity

...To me, a true Butler is someone who makes others feel completely at ease, and that means seeing to their needs before his or her own. A Butler has a strong desire to be of service to others and he never ceases to learn. Service to others is rewarding and generous, and there's much to be learned from the Butler by adopting a spirit of generosity and selflessness with anyone in your life.

Discretion separates a good Butler from a great one. A great Butler has the ability to go about his or her work almost invisibly. In fact, invisibility is a trait that to this day continues to be much sought after in the service industry...the very best Butlers blend into the environment so much that they become a part of it, allowing occupants of the room a sense of privacy and security even when they are not alone...The Butler must be interested in understanding his employer's needs and requirements, but he is never on show or expected to be the focal point of attention. He should, at all times, maintain a calm and demure demeanor. He should always allow his employer to be the center of attention...Another skill that clearly defines the Butler is the ability to anticipate. Alas, the skill is not easily taught. It's innate or it's not. But I must tell you that the ability to anticipate your employer's needs — whether you are a Butler or not — is a powerful one that trumps almost any other...The professional Butler should not be the center of attention, but many, even today, are in the privileged position of both watching history unfold and orchestrating events behind the scenes...Though a Butler will never tell, he may watch the evening news at the end of the day and think to himself with pride, *I was part of the team that allowed that moment to happen.* For me, this feeling is my private reward and something of which I am deeply proud.

Private Service Profile: Robert Hayman

Job Duties and Responsibilities

"Working as Butler, Chef, Private Flight Attendant and Chauffeur I have always enjoyed serving others with great alacrity. I have cleaned toilets and served Royalty, flown to Paris to fetch an expensive cat only to return, by no fault of my own, to find it was the wrong one, cleaned up after a teenage drinking party that went South, taught etiquette to the children, planned last minute dinner parties for 20 with no notice, waited 15 hours for Aunt Mabel's delayed flight to bring her to Thanksgiving dinner and held the hand of my Mrs. when she was frightened about her surgery that was scheduled the next day. I also brought in the mail and took out the trash too!"

How did I get started in my career?

"I worked at The University Club in 1980, a fine dining supper club in Jacksonville, Florida. I was asked by a member if I could serve in their home and play the "Butler" role at one of their formal dinners. I said; "YES!", and when answering the phone that night at their home the caller asked me; "Well, who is this"?... and I replied; "I am The Anderson's Butler Ma'am, my name is Robert, do you wish to leave a message?" I continued to offer my service to other members of the club and finally landed a full time position as a Butler to a wonderful family. I continued to take courses in house management, cooking, wine, bookkeeping and time management and the rest is history."

What do I like most about my job?

"Dealing with difficult situations, making it happen when you think it's impossible. Spontaneous last minute travel plans with an hour to pack, coming to the rescue. Flying around the world on a Falcon 2000 or a 737 Boeing Business Jet. Teaching etiquette to the children and helping with their homework. Wine cellar inventory and the samples that come with that. Shopping for the Holidays and decorating the house. Achieving a time honored family recipe to perfection and serving it. Dressing up in my cutaway and white gloves to answer the door. Sitting on the edge of my bed at the end of the day and thanking GOD for my talents and the ability to serve and share them with those I serve."

What is the Most Important Skill or Ability for you to be Successful at your Job?

"Service Heart! I have one. It's something you are born with and something that grows when you are aware of it and nurture it. As it grows it gives you increased patience, consideration, love, kindness, gentility and sympathy to others. Service Heart is essential to anyone in the service industry, if you truly want to serve from the heart! It also helps to be a great organizer, planner, a maker of lists and follow up, a clever cook and a frugal meal planner. The skills of knowing when to participate and when to be silent. Anticipation of others needs and fulfilling them without notice, gently and quietly. Above all the most important ability is your etiquette and Service Heart.

A Brief Example...

When you have a Service Heart you don't see a situation as a problem, but instead as a challenge which YOU are in charge and will make the difference. It's about aligning your heart with your brain and emotions and acting upon the best interest for that particular situation. It's always truthful and fair."

Favorite Story

"I recently moved back to the Tampa Bay Area, Brandon, Florida to be specific. I decided to take a part time job at The Bonefish Grill in Brandon. When I arrived at The Fish, as we call it, I met my new Manager and Owner Mr. Bruce Roberts. During the interview for 'Guest Service Associate' he told me what he was looking for. I told him very little about myself and tried to show him my impressive resume. He said; what's that? And I said; 'That's my resume!' I pushed my resume toward him and he pushed it back toward me and said...'I don't need that...' I was crushed that he didn't want to look at my impressive resume.

And, then he said; 'I look for heart and a smile that impresses me, if I don't feel it or see it I move on...Can you start tomorrow?' It was and is the greatest compliment of my life! I am blessed."

Personal Assistant

Title

Commonly nicknamed "PA" (Except in Hollywood / Los Angeles where PA is used for Production Assistant) this position may be referred to as a Social Secretary, Family Assistant, or Executive

Assistant, depending on the base location and the daily functions. This position usually is the closest to the family or boss on a personal level, and often one of the most mentally demanding due to ever-changing roles.

Environment

A Personal Assistant is typically home based either in the employer's home office or a separate room of the home for the purpose. In a more executive situation the assistant will work from the employer's corporate office to help with business, personal, and home duties. At times, depending on the level of in-home service necessary, this can be a live-in job.

Functions

Of all positions in the home, the Personal Assistant can mean the most things to different people. Some very specific roles could be:

-Social Coordinator for the owner, maintaining a calendar and travel arrangements as a full-time job.
-Office Assistant, handling the bills, correspondence, office organization, and errands.
-Family Assistant, performing the role and duties of a House Manager.
-Gentleman's Gentleman or Lady's Lady, providing personal service and Valet functions, and often traveling with the employer.
-Personal shopper.
-Business Manager.
-Executive Assistant – handling more business or office/secretarial related duties.

More than likely these days a Personal Assistant will encompass all of the above! Especially in a live-in scenario, the Assistant can become simply the "right hand" of the employer, doing whatever is necessary to ensure their overall comfort and success. The Personal Assistant could end up paying bills in the morning, attending an afternoon business meeting, and preparing a sit down dinner for 10 by nightfall, all while responding to dozens of emails and booking a flight for the principal!

Qualification

Personal Assistant roles will require the most diversified range of qualifications. This position is heavily dictated by the specific functions needed by an employer. Most PA's come from an administrative background with very sharply honed business and communication skills, often mixing office assistance and personal tasks for the boss and his or her family. Since the relationship is so close with a PA and their employer, personality and discretion are high on the list of desired qualities. Many Assistants eventually must act on behalf of their employer in business and social settings. They must represent the desired image in public and protect the interests of the employer and family at all times. Some PA's travel with their boss and work closely as a confidant, knowing secrets never to be told! Valuable qualifications include:

-Office and computer expertise.
-Top writing and speaking ability.
-Complete dedication to the service and success of the employer.
-Well rounded knowledge of social, cultural, and business practices.
-Resourceful, "get it done no matter what" attitude and performance.
-Extremely independent self-starter. Anticipates and fills the needs of the boss seamlessly and without being asked twice.
-Creative and intuitive thinking and problem solving.
-Very, very, very resourceful.
-Highest levels of tolerance, selflessness, and patience.
-Well-traveled.
-Discreet and trustworthy above all else.

The career Personal Assistant understands the complete abandonment of their own goals and personal fulfillment while working for their employer. This is where most first time PA's can fail miserably. It takes a unique attitude and dedication to be a top Personal Assistant, found in few individuals. Because of this, past performance and personal recommendations are the keys to finding a truly valuable assistant.

Compensation

Typical salary range is $60,000 - $100,000. Again we see a very broad range of salary based on the level of experience and scope of duties performed. Additional benefits may include fully paid housing, automobile, insurance, paid travel, clothing allowance, and more. "Fringe benefits" can be huge with a celebrity or frequent traveler, gaining access to people, events, and places some only dream of!

Expert's View - Bonnie Low-Kramen

As one of the best known Private Service Professionals in our industry, Bonnie Low Kramen is a role model and fantastic example of a career Personal Assistant. Bonnie has graciously offered her insights and personal story to educate and join with others in the Assistant field.

Bonnie's Bio:

Bonnie Low-Kramen's career for 25 years was as the Personal Assistant to celebrity couple Olympia Dukakis (Academy Award, Moonstruck, Steel Magnolias) and Louis Zorich (Mad About You.) Respected as a leader in the profession, she is a co-founder and former President of New York Celebrity Assistants (NYCA), a networking and support organization for New York-based celebrity assistants. Bonnie has written the book on the subject – Be the Ultimate Assistant, A celebrity assistant's secrets to working with any high-powered employer, and has written many articles which have been published in magazines and newsletters around the world. She is a popular speaker at conferences and meetings. Committed to affecting positive change in the American workplace, Bonnie is now teaching weekend and one-day workshops for assistants in major U.S. cities. "The time is right for more structured training of Personal Assistants as the demand for broadly skilled excellent assistants is pressing and immediate in today's workplace. Education is the key to raising the bar of professionalism." Bonnie's work with Olympia Dukakis included close involvement with the Academy Award win for Moonstruck, the 1988 presidential campaign of Michael Dukakis, travel around the world to places such as Sydney, London, Alaska and Prague and numerous awards shows and benefits. A New Jersey native, Bonnie holds a B.A. degree from Rutgers University in English and Theatre. Her website is www.bonnielowkramen.com

Description of my position:

For 25 years, I worked as the Personal Assistant to actors Olympia Dukakis and Louis Zorich. My job duties were 50% personal, 50% business. I was a PA/HM and as such, I supervised the housekeeper and coordinated repairs and renovations. I worked out of Louis and Olympia's home. The responsibilities ranged from scheduling and travel arrangements to reviewing contracts to handling medical insurance billing to paying bills to personal shopping. Everyone in their lives, including family and friends, knew to contact me to get in touch with them. I was on call 24/7 and scheduled my vacations around theirs. I took my phone with me to the movies and the grocery store and on vacation. I was the liaison with the accountant, lawyer, and banker. Part of my job was to help them buy and sell 4 homes including coordinating the moves, furnishings, and maintenance. I organized parties and weddings. I did not always travel with Olympia but on more complicated projects, I did go.

How did I get started?:

How I got started in my career was through networking. I am from New Jersey but worked as the Box Office Manager at the Alley Theatre in Houston for a year. A colleague from the Alley introduced me to Olympia Dukakis who was the Producing Artistic Director of the Whole Theatre in Montclair, NJ.

Favorite Things:

What I loved about my job was that no two days were never the same. I also enjoyed the wide range of responsibilities mainly because Olympia Dukakis preferred to delegate everything she could in order to have the freedom to pursue her work. Olympia knew how to fully utilize a PA!

What it Takes:

The most important skill for me to be successful was my ability to "read" situations and to immediately re-prioritize based on the needs. More than anything, a personal assistant's role is to organize the chaos on a daily basis and I had a pretty easy time with this. I call it "administrative triage." Keeping calm in a crisis was definitely a strong suit.

The Good Times:

One of my favorite stories was from the presidential race of 1988. Olympia was committed to helping her cousin Michael Dukakis in his campaign. They often made appearances together. One day they were in a limo heading to an interview in NYC. As usual, Olympia had her schedule all typed out so she knew what to expect for the day. Michael questioned their next move so Olympia consulted the schedule that I had prepared. She told Michael emphatically, "If Bonnie says this is where we are going, that's where we are supposed to go!" And yes, I was right. What I love about this story was the complete trust that Olympia and I had between us which just got stronger as the years went on.

The Bad Times:

I've made some pretty major mistakes in my career. There are so many moving parts when you work as a PA, it would be impossible for this not to be the case. I remember the sick feeling in the pit of my stomach on the morning after Olympia has given a speech in front of 300 people. I had been responsible for all the details of the trip including preparing the speech. To my horror, I had given her the wrong one and she did not figure it out until she was on stage and she was forced to improvise. We discussed what had gone wrong and I apologized. And I never again gave her a wrong speech! If you are to succeed as a personal assistant, these kinds of mistakes only get to happen once.

Career Reflections:

When Olympia read this piece, she said, "Do you remember when you wouldn't talk at meetings? I would say, when is the tall one going to talk? That certainly changed." It's true. It took at least two months to feel confident enough to speak up in a meeting because I was afraid of appearing stupid or ill-informed. I realize I've had many of those days too and some pretty recently. Fear can be paralyzing, debilitating, and demoralizing. It's an all too common problem for many in private service.

The profession looks glamorous on the surface and it does have its fabulous moments. It has also meant sleepless nights, long and stressful days, difficult people, demanding deadlines, headaches, and tense conversations. Too many tasks and too little time in which to do them. It is impossible to not make lots of mistakes given the detail-orientation of this work. The trick has been to try to only let them happen once and to take responsibility when they do.

I learned a great deal in 25 years. Olympia and Louis have been my mentors, teachers, and friends and many times, I to them. I continued to discover how to sustain a long-term working relationship by learning from my own mistakes and theirs. (Celebrities are human too.) The whole thing is in constant motion, a living, breathing entity. Nothing, including a job description, can be engraved in stone. Everything is up for grabs because life happens and we needed to stay open and responsive to the natural shifts that take place simply because we are human. The mistake is to fight those shifts.

We have gone through some of life's biggest milestones together and witnessed each other's lives. The birth of my son Adam in 1988 just three weeks before Olympia won the Oscar. I was grateful that Best Supporting Actress was the first award announced that night because Adam was in my arms as I watched the TV with pride − and then we both went to sleep. My divorce. The deaths of both of our mothers. Opening nights, movie premieres, award shows, and quiet times in hospital rooms. 25 years of following the trials and tribulations of our children and families and all the while traveling all over the world and managing to stay closely connected whether by phone, fax, or email.

Looking back, I now possess the thing I did not have on that first day of work. I found my voice. As the years have gone by, it's gotten stronger and clearer and I actually have quite a lot to say. My work enabled me to figure out the things I cared about and empowered me to do something about them.

In 2004, I self-published a book called, "Be the Ultimate Assistant, A celebrity assistant's secrets to working with any high-powered employer." It was my way to support personal assistants and administrative professionals all around the world and while it's far from a best-seller, I have done what I set out to do. In the most recent edition of the book, I added a chapter called "Gender in the Workplace" because so much about finding my voice had to do with figuring out what happens between women and men in the world and in the workplace. The relationship between staff and employers in today's workplace and especially private service is of particular interest to me. This subject has become a passion and something of a mission to support other private service professionals to find their voices too.

This subject leads to the issues of respect, appreciation, fair compensation, self-esteem, assertiveness, and positive confrontation with co-workers and employers. We must figure out how to effectively deal with bullying without losing our jobs or self-respect. Many people are having a tough time working in both private homes and offices. Abusive and destructive situations exist and are made worse by the tight job market. I see it, I hear it, and it is important to try to deal with it head-on.

Perhaps part of why my work with Olympia and Louis thrived for 25 years is because they supported me to pursue these passions. When I gave Olympia the final draft of the book to offer her carte blanche to take out anything she did not like, she handed it back and said, "Don't change a word."

At the beginning, Olympia, Louis and I did not dare to think forward about how long our relationship would last. Olympia and I both had a need. I needed a job and in her late 50's, Olympia was suddenly busier and in more demand than ever before due in large part to winning the Academy Award in 1988 for her role in Norman Jewison's "Moonstruck" with Cher and Nicolas Cage. Olympia followed up that movie with "Steel Magnolias," "Mr. Holland's Opus," and "Tales of the City." As her personal assistant, I can tell you that since "Moonstruck" the phone never stopped ringing. 25 years later, it's slightly quieter now but that is only because of e-mail.

Communication – frequent, clear, consistent, and accurate – is key. There are so many more choices than there were in 1986. Consider that when Olympia was nominated for an Academy Award in 1987, we managed the entire Oscar race without cell phones or computers. Can you even imagine it? At the same time, Olympia was helping her cousin Michael Dukakis run for President of the United States by doing as much press as possible with him and without him. That meant scheduling private planes, limos, hair and makeup artists all by telephone. Sometimes six events in one day for several days in a row. Complicated, high-level coordination was required without the benefit of current technology. The point is that we got it done. Don't get me wrong, I love the way technology helps us with our work and I hope Olympia gets nominated for another Oscar for many reasons, not the least of which is that she and her new assistant (who I hired) would do it so much better this time.

Personal assistants do whatever it takes to get the job done and that is a very broad spectrum. Now I have the privilege of teaching those who aspire to be "ultimate assistants." There has been too little support for Personal Assistants so that is why I created training classes which can be done in person or virtually. It's my way of staying connected and giving back to a profession that blessed me in so many ways through the years.

Personal / Private Chef or Household Cook

Title

There is not much variation in the titles for Chef and Cook. The more formal of the two, Chef, is likely to indicate formal chef training in school or through apprenticeship under another Head Chef, usually in a restaurant. Household cook may indicate a less formal position or be part of a combination of responsibilities in one job. Here is another perfect example of the job being descried based on the employer's needs. Whether they want a personal "Chef" to do formal, five-star, restaurant caliber meals and entertaining, a "Gourmet Cook" to prepare delicious daily lunch and dinner, or a "Household Cook" for simple family meals, the tastes of the employer dictate service levels. For this guide, the skills and descriptions below are based on the more formal role of a Private Chef.

Environment

The Chef has one place to call home: The Kitchen. The typical household will have only one kitchen, but a larger home or estate designed for entertaining will include two or more, in order to separate staff or caterers from the family kitchen. Occasionally the Chef will also provide services to the employer's place of business either via delivery or working in a corporate kitchen.

Functions

A true Chef position within the private service environment is dedicated solely to the culinary needs of the home. The Chef will be responsible for menu preparation, stocking of all food and related ingredients, pantry and refrigerator rotation and cleanliness, and arrangement of meal service. Often family meals are served by the cooks themselves, but a formal dinner with guests is more likely to be waited on by a Butler or other service staff. Some variations in duties for a Chef or Cook are based on the schedule and eating habits of the family they serve. For instance, one family may have only dinner as a sit down meal, while another may eat three scheduled meals per day with formal service. Most common is a Lunch and Dinner schedule with some time devoted to shopping and creating a few prepared items for the refrigerator to be eaten at breakfast or between meals. Additionally, Chefs may be required at times to manage an entertainment function where additional kitchen staff is necessary. A catering company is often brought in for large parties and is assisted or directed by the family's head Chef. Another family may choose to travel with their cook to other residences, yachts, planes, and sometimes even in hotels. Lastly, perhaps a more recent variation of duties might find a Chef taking on household management functions. Though possible in a home with a smaller service structure and less frequent dining, we never recommend combining the true full time Chef with other unrelated household positions. Either or both roles will suffer.

Qualification

Ideally the best Chef or Cook for a home will have past experience within similar homes. As with all of the other positions, past performance is the best indicator of future success. Many Chefs make a successful transition to private service from fine restaurants, while others may have developed their skills from years of cooking in combination with another domestic position or assisting another Chef. Either way, important traits include:

-Well rounded cooking technique. Knowing just one item such as baking or sauces may not produce great overall meals.

-Wine and food pairing knowledge is a plus.

-Creative menu planning skills.

-Knowledge of entertaining and catering service.

-Presentation skills based on the formal level of the household or entertaining.

-Excellent time management and attention to detail.

-Proper sanitary practices and knowledgeable selection of fresh ingredients.

-Good listening and communication skills to hear and react to the particular tastes of the family.

-Familiarity or expertise in any family diet preferences or restrictions. (i.e. spa cuisine, vegetarian, comfort foods, etc.)

Once again the main idea is to find an employee that is or can be "customized" to your home. (A French pastry chef won't be much good to a family who loves Indian food!) Also be sure the candidate is comfortable in a home environment and enjoyable to be around while dining, which should always be a peaceful, stress-free experience. One of the employment scenarios unique to Chefs is that a trial of their cooking can be evaluated in short order! (Pardon the pun.) Chefs will always participate in a sample cooking trial for a potential employer. An agency can help arrange this as part of the interview process, and clients typically are charged a "day rate" plus food costs. It's a great scenario for everyone to evaluate the match.

Compensation

Common salary requirements for household Chefs fall in the range of $40,000 – $100,000+ based on the expertise and schedule requirements. Renowned and very successful candidates can earn far higher based on their salary history and the tastes of the employer.

Travel requirements are a key factor in the salary package. A Chef can easily be a live-in or live-out position and benefits are usually included with the salary package.

Private Service Profile: Mike Neylan

Job duties and responsibilities:
"My job consists of planning daily meals for my client. This includes shopping, prepping, cooking and serving. Other duties are cleaning the kitchen and pantry areas. Keeping all kitchen appliances in working order is also part of my job. If a repairs needs to be made I notify my client or repair people. Another part of my job is to handle any special events for my clients' family, friends or business needs. I notify wait staff and bartenders of upcoming events. I also find out if any guests have any food related allergies or special dietary needs (diabetic-gluten free-dairy free etc.) I am also constantly coming up with new menu ideas to keep the meals fresh and exciting."

How did I get started in my career?
"26 years ago I graduated from culinary school and worked in high-end restaurants and bakeries in the Greenwich, CT area. I then opened my own Private Jet Catering company supplying in-flight catering for corporate, celebrity and sport team clients. Making the transition to being a private Chef was an easy decision because I was essentially a Private Chef to my high profile private jet clients for many years already."

What do I like most about my job?
"The most rewarding and best part of my job is to be creative. Going to local farmers markets and stores and picking

the freshest, highest quality ingredients and turning them into a great meal is very rewarding. The controlled chaos that each new day brings is also a challenge I enjoy. No two days are exactly the same, and unlike some who stare at the clock all day waiting to leave, I glance at the clock occasionally and wonder where all the time has gone. The most rewarding aspect of my job is seeing the expressions on my clients face when they taste the food I prepared."

What is the most important skill or ability for me to be successful at my job?

"Besides having an overall knowledge and skill of many different cooking styles and cuisines after preparing food for clients from all over the world, I have to pay particular attention to detail. From planning the menus and shopping, to prep and actual cooking of the meals, everything has to be perfect. The most important ability is to listen to the client. What they want is the most important detail. I would not have been so successful in my career if I did not anticipate my clients' needs and deliver them on a consistent basis."

What is a favorite story about a unique job situation?

"One of my most memorable job situations was when I was doing Private Jet catering. One of my client's assistants thought she had faxed in and order for a flight her boss was taking. When she called a few hours before the flight to make a revision was when I realized the error. What normally would have been a day long prepping and cooking suddenly needed to be prepared and delivered in less than 3 hours. Utilizing my trusted supplier reps, I had them deliver the needed specialty meats and seafood. My staff and I managed to get everything done and on its way to the private airport. Usually when food is prepared for an in-flight catering it is put in a refrigerator in the hangar for the flight attendants to take on board. Because of the timing the plane was already on the runway. I drove the food right onto the runway (this being a private airport this was possible). I handed off the food to the flight attendants and the flight was on its way. One important thing I have learned from my experience as a business owner and being a private chef is that no matter what happens, the most important thing is to stay calm and handle the situation. Being flexible and able to take control of what might seem to be a terrible situation is an important part of being a Private Chef."

Domestic Couple

Title

The position commonly called "Domestic Couple" or simply "Couple" refers to a married or partnered team that fill two or more roles in a household. Any other specific functions they perform can alter the name, but it is always two people working as a team. For instance, "Estate Management Team", "Housekeeping Team", etc. For this section, we'll use the simplest title, "Couple."

Environment

A Couple can fill many types of roles either as part of a larger management team or as the "do-it-all" employees with no other staff. This creates many scenarios for employment of a Couple, from a small, single residence to multiple property estates of all sizes. We have worked with Couples in every capacity, from both employees as house cleaners to both as administrative staff in a shared Estate Manager role. We've even seen Chef teams handling the very busy culinary and entertaining aspects of a client's lifestyle.

Functions

Couple job descriptions and duties span the entire list of job requirements in any combination. The following are some of the common roles associated with Couples:

-Household Manager / Chef
-Butler / Chef
-Chef / Housekeeper
-Housekeeper / Groundskeeper
-Housekeeper / Handyman
-Housekeeper / Cook
-Chef / Sous Chef

The main idea here is that any combination is possible based on the employer's property and service needs. Usually the Couple is employed to cover many other tasks in addition to their emphasis. It is not uncommon to see a Cook / Housekeeping team also responsible for items such as driving, childcare, laundry, home office and personal assistance, errands, shopping, etc. The Couple normally works the same hours and schedules days off either both at the same time or one day separate, one day together. Once again, the roles can be formal, informal, or mixed based on the family.

Qualification

The important considerations in all Couple positions are flexibility and range of skills. A couple assigned to specific functions at a high level must be trained or experienced in those areas. There are so many variables within the combinations that employers should look at each role as if they were hiring for the individual positions. However, some basic traits have shown greater success in the performance and longevity of a Couple in any variety of roles. They are:

-Strong, lengthy personal relationship.

-History of successfully working together full time.

-Demonstrated flexibility in skills and schedules.

-Lifestyles compatible with the work schedule, living quarters, and geography.

-Ability to work as a team or independently as necessary.

-Time management and project completion skills.

The overall fit for a Couple will have many factors in common with other positions, but the added dynamic of the relationship between the pair can prove disastrous! Make sure that personalities "jive" with the family and any other staff before making this hire. One of the other downsides to this hire is the potential to lose both employees at the same time. When leaving the job for any reason, both positions need to be filled again and the client may find themselves "short staffed" during the transition. Over time we've seen that the benefits of a professional service couple far outweigh the potential negatives.

Compensation

Couples' pay scales and benefits have a broad range considering the different functions and levels of professionalism required. Salaries are seen as low as $50,000 and as high as $200,000 plus for the team. At the top of the range, Couples tend to earn slightly less than two equally trained and experienced individuals in the same roles, a benefit to the family employing the team. Living arrangements are almost always separate from the main home or off-site. Insurance benefits and use of an automobile are also common.

Support Staff

The following positions may be found in smaller homes individually, but for the purpose of discussing estates and households that require a management structure, these will be considered "support" staff. A good Estate Manager or House Manager will be familiar with the techniques necessary to do most of the "support" functions and will be able to hire and train accordingly.

Housekeeper or Houseman

Reporting to an Estate or House Manager, the Housekeeper or Houseman is responsible for cleaning and maintenance duties in the household. This may include dusting, vacuuming, bathroom cleaning, floor care, bedroom preparation, laundry, linens, care of silver, crystal and other fine or fragile items. The Houseman position might also encompass some of the more physically challenging items like cleaning high windows, lighting, ceilings, and operating floor care equipment. Other areas can include automobile and vehicle care, various related errands outside of the home, supply shopping and inventory control, and more.

The management level of this position may be referred to as Executive Housekeeper when the employee directs his or her own support staff. This title may cover several duties including hands-on house cleaning, hiring, training, and managing other house cleaning staff, and providing a mix of organizing and managing projects throughout the house. Like the Butler or House manager titles, the Executive Housekeeper has grown more ambiguous as a role in a variety of households. Recently we have had many requests for the expanded role of an Executive Housekeeper who is a form of Household Manager in a smaller or less complex home. The only downside, as in all combination roles, is the potential to overlap too many responsibilities and as a result, some functions get less care than others. Mixing cooking with other positions is the most frequently out of balance. The actual functions will be the most important to clarify in constructing a successful job description.

Private Service Profile: Elizabeth Stone, Executive Housekeeper

Elizabeth is a currently employed service professional in the Chicago area. She has had a number of years in high level private service. Her favorite household role can best be described as an Executive Housekeeper and is a nice example of the many different talents this role might employ.

Description of Job, Duties and Responsibilities of My Position:

"I was employed primarily as the first floor Executive Housekeeper with a duality, and whenever necessary, as a Personal Secretary to the lady of the house. Also because of my background in art history, it was my position to properly care for the various paintings and sculptures that were throughout the house."

How Did I Get Started in My Career?

"I was the manager and event planner for a small, but very elegant restaurant. Many affluent families chose this restaurant for entertaining because of the classic architectural motif of the dining room. The restaurant also had a superb chef who was highly thought of and very well versed. Because of the intimacy of the dining room and the demand for specialized attention, I became friendly with a particular diner who was very fond of our establishment. After several months of our acquaintance, she asked me if I would possibly be interested in working on her estate as an Executive Housekeeper, which I accepted."

What is the Most Important Skill or Ability for Me to be Successful at My Job?

"I feel that the reason this particular woman approached me to work on her estate and ultimately was pleased with her choice of me, was due to the fact that she knew I would be very respectful of her home and her family. I also feel that I had an understanding of their utmost need for discretion and respect for her and her family's privacy in all matters."

Tell a Favorite Story About a Unique Job Situation or Employer:

"The lady of the house ran a very formal household retaining much of the old style ways of entertaining. Preparing for a dinner party was incredibly detail orientated. Part of my position was to confer with the chef in deciding upon an appropriate menu, which I would then type up for the guests who were attending the function. There would be a variety of exquisite linens and various china and crystal services to choose from for the various dinner parties. Each dinner party had a different motif, whether it be color or theme, which had to be subtly infused into the presentation. The creation of ambiance is really an art in itself, so this involved a good deal of thought and expertise. The estate's personal chef was a former Norwegian Cruise Line chef. The Lady of the House and Chef were very fond of serving many elaborate dishes that have fallen out of favor in today's society. These social events were very beautifully executed and I feel that I have learned more from these two women than I could from any culinary institute. Over the course of my employment, my employer enjoyed relating stories of her very interesting childhood and adolescence. Her father had been a US Ambassador and the family had been stationed in India and parts of Asia during the twenties and thirties. Her memories were really quite fascinating and I will never forget them."

Laundress

This one just about speaks for itself. As a very specialized role in a home, the Laundress will take care of and oversee all the laundering requirements. This entails personal wardrobe, linens, towels, and other items requiring the service. She may also arrange for any dry cleaning or special laundering from outside vendors. The Laundress should have knowledge of all related equipment and specialty care of materials. They will have to establish relationships with appropriate vendors and know how to respond to all cleaning emergencies involving fabrics and clothing.

Chauffeur

This is another very specific role for a larger or very busy family estate. A chauffeur will drive family and guests upon request and will also be responsible for the maintenance of all vehicles. A Chauffeur at certain levels may have security and emergency driving training as well. The best will know the area "like the back of their hand" and will quickly make route adjustments based on traffic and security elements. A Chauffeur, or Driver, will also need to understand the utmost levels of service, manners, and confidentiality, as they will be in close contact with employers and guests during times of extended casual conversation.

Gardener / Groundskeeper

The head Gardener or Groundskeeper is responsible for the upkeep and appearance of the entire grounds including landscaping, pools, ponds or lakes, flowers (inside and out), driveways, paths, lighting, irrigation, etc. They may also supervise outside contractors or other workers for the maintenance duties. Specialty positions include knowledge of ecosystems, lawn and garden equipment, plant, flower, and grass varieties, and perhaps an expert niche such as Japanese Gardens. This role can be very distinguished and expert level at times.

If the property is used as a showcase then the Gardener's operations will be as significant as the House Manager. At the higher level the Gardener position requires extensive training and experience.

There are many other jobs on a large estate property with varying titles and duties. It all depends on how elaborate any particular life-style activities are for the client. Some of them are:

Valet
Gentleman's Gentleman
Lady's Maid
Governess / Nanny / Babysitter
Tutor / Home School Teacher
Social Secretary
Shopping and Gift Manager
Home or Personal Security
Personal Trainer
Private Pilot or Captain
Pet Nanny or Dog Walker
Hunting Guide / Gamekeeper

Additional Private Service Profiles: Julie Mills, Personal Assistant

Job duties:

"I'm currently working as a Personal Assistant. Of all the positions I have been in, it is still my favorite. My basic weekly duties include the typical errands, such as the post office, banking, household supply run, shipping, personal purchases and returns. I also take care of all the vehicles and pets, travel on occasion to the Principal's second home to work, do the packing and unpacking for their travels, booking and dealing with all the contractors, supervising the household staff, helping with special events, all the clothing care, and lots of research.. There are some office duties, and overall really just keeping the house running like a well-oiled machine."

How I got started:

"I moved from Sydney, Australia to Vancouver, Canada in 1986 and my first job was as a Nanny for 3 children under the age of 5, housekeeper & cook. She was an OB/Gyn and he was a Pilot, so I was basically on call 24/7. A typical day was from 7am - 7pm. It didn't take me long to be hired by a family, as I had been babysitting & cooking since the age of 12, plus my parents instilled in me both hard work ethics, and having high standards in all I did. Since then I have also worked in Toronto, Portland, Seattle, & now Nashville; as a House & Property Manager, Estate Manager, Private Chef, & Personal Assistant....or combos of these."

What I like most:

"Like most people who do this job....I love the variety! I love the fact that every day is different, so I never get bored. I love taking care of people too. Basically this job suits all of my personality traits....like reliable, resourceful, organized, trustworthy, flexible, hospitable, creative, a multi-tasker, & self starter. Also I NEVER think I'm above doing anything I'm asked to do....no matter what my title is!! If you don't have a "can-do" personality - this is not the type of job for you! Oh, & I never let them see me stressed. Not that it happens much, but they need to feel like I have everything under control at all times. Oh, and I have to be honest....the perks are really nice too!"

What it takes to succeed:

"I'm a perfectionist & that sits very well with my clients! Also, I have a good memory. A client can ask you to do a dozen things "on the fly" and if you don't have some way to write it down - you better have a great memory, as they don't like to repeat themselves! As for being a perfectionist, chances are you either work for one, or you work for someone who is not....but really wants & needs you to be that way, in order to keep their homes, lives, etc. organized. I also pride myself in being very flexible and reliable. A client may want you to be available to do anything or go anywhere - sometimes on a moment's notice. Here's another... it doesn't matter how good you are at your job if there is no chemistry between you and your client. I don't think you will be in the position very long if that's the case. You are with these people day in and day out, knowing, seeing, and hearing very private and sometimes intimate things. If there is no chemistry, there is no trust, and without those two things I don't think you can do your job well. You must be one step ahead of them - which is another very important quality."

Favorite stories:

"My best perk was getting $20,000 from a client for my 'bonus', so I flew my husband & step kids to Australia to meet my family and travel around. I've also flown in private jets, been picked up in a stretch limo just to deliver an envelope, driven all sorts of high end, beautiful vehicles, been given tickets to shows, stayed in my clients homes for personal vacations, been allowed to take family & friends on free vacations, given clothes, jewelry, and stayed in beautiful hotels, and more.

I have had the opportunity to work for some very high profile people in the music industry, which has been fun & very interesting. In fact, every performer I have wanted to work for in Nashville, I have been hired by! I believe that if you want something bad enough, and are good at what you do and believe in yourself, it can happen! Or....I've just been very lucky!

I have custom designed the interior of a brand new Range Rover being shipped from Europe, sewn my client into her gown before an awards show, flown to NYC for a day with a singer's master tape of her whole new unreleased album so that a film company could download one song to be used in their upcoming release, helped move and set up homes before the owner arrived, driven the dog to the vacation homes, slept in a client's bed when her husband was out of town so she could go to sleep and not feel alone and scared, figured out the best way to transport an entire frozen cow from upstate NY to Nashville within 12 hours, shopped for clothes for Whitney Houston when she came into town unexpectedly to stay with my client, cooked for a private party where some of the city's best celebrities showed up, found real reindeer and elves for a Christmas party, and planned a wedding in Martha's Vineyard – without ever going there."

Additional Private Service Profiles: Onna Lil Salerno, Executive Housekeeper

How I got started:

"I started working as a housekeeper in a private home in Atlanta, Georgia in 1983. I didn't even speak proper English, but the Butler in the House Manager told me two things: pass around the hors d'oeuvres, and smile all the time, (they will not know you can't speak English). That was the first time in my life that someone made me feel so degraded. At that moment I knew the urgency to find a school to learn English right away. I was fascinated with the job; I felt it was a castle and I had the privilege to work in the castle.

But my English was so bad! There was a big party the day I started working, and a lady asked me for an 'ashtray' and I brought her sugar! She looked at me and laughed, so in my mind I was already enrolled in school. Because I was so in love with my job, I made a commitment to learn as much as possible to be a Butler one day. I enrolled in the school the following day and every day I learned a new word. I loved the fact that everybody loved my accent; that was a complement for me. I started reading about how to clean every corner of every room. Fine furniture, wood floors, silverware, etc. I learned everything because I loved to learn and I wanted to be the best in what I was doing."

What I like most:

"I love to serve, to be needed. I consider this my career. It took me so many years to learn everything I know. Almost

25 years it took me to learn all the details, all the secrets. It makes me happy to take care of other people. When they recognize that I can solve their problems it makes me feel better every day. I worked for several residences through the years, all the houses are different. I learned new things all the time and I took the best of all of them. The feeling of being needed is very important; it means that what you are doing you're doing right. When I come to work my mind is transformed, it's like I become another person. I have a script every day, and every day is different. I feel like a movie star! You solve everybody's problems, and just act! It made me so happy to see my boss' face looking around and seeing that everything is perfectly immaculate the way she wanted it. Once the job is done, I start a new chapter. You have to be prepared, every day is a challenge and you have to be confident and patient. You have to be a team leader and have to have a good eye for details, good presentation skills and work ethic. You have to be prepared that every day you are going to have different kinds of situations. To be a housekeeper is not an easy job, you have to know what you are doing and be proud of your work as well."

What it takes to succeed:

"Discretion, personal responsibility, punctuality, adaptability, trust, integrity, and most importantly be willing to work hard. I have excellent computer skills, knowledge of various software programs, so I also took care of the daily agenda, made reservations and organized special events."

Favorite story:

"I have thousands of stories, but this is the story about one of my jobs in Atlanta, Georgia, with one of the most prestigious families that I've had the privilege of working with.

They had two children when I started, 2 years old and 4. I was one of the housekeepers and after lunch time I was as their nanny. Taking care of the children was so fun, they loved me and I loved them. They taught me English and I taught them Spanish. It was during summer break, both parents were working late everyday so I stayed with the children. One night we had an intruder in the house and I was so in shock that my natural instinct as a mother was to protect the children. The intruders were looking for money and jewelry. The little girl told one of the men, 'please don't do anything to my mother!' When I heard that, I started talking and screaming in English; it was like a miracle, I don't know from where the words came from. They destroyed the house looking for money; the rest of the employees ran away and left me alone with the children. When the parents showed up I was shaking but always showed the children I was very strong and firm, repeating 'I am here nothing is going to happen, don't worry.' Inside I was dying, I was so afraid. The parents saw the children were fine and asked me, where are the rest of the people? I said I didn't know, maybe they left. That day they fired all of them and I gave me the position as a House Manager and a very good raise. The children are now 15 and 19 and still send me cards in Christmas and my birthday. Every chance I can I go to Atlanta and make sure to visit their home. Good memories and one of the best experiences of my life!"

Additional Private Service Profiles: Estella Ferrer, House Manager

How I got started:
"I got started in this career as a fluke. I have my Culinary Arts degree and have had my own restaurant and catering

company. I was helping out a friend that had a commercial cleaning company when an employee called out sick. This was an afterhours job so there was no chance of running into anyone. I was cleaning out the office and there was one person working late. I had no idea who she was. I asked if it was ok to go in and clean she said yes of course. After about 20 minutes in her office she stopped me and said, I want you to come work for me! I laughed it off and said, 'I am just helping out a friend tonight.' She insisted and asked that I go to her home and see if I would like to be her Estate Manager. After speaking with her and seeing her home she made me an offer I could not refuse, so the rest is history."

What I like most about my job:

"Every day is different. I have yet to have any day be the same old day after day. It's a fast thinking, quick to adjust mindset and attitude. You do many tasks and there are some surprises as well. I enjoy making sure their home is perfect and all is running well. No request is ever impossible. I enjoy the fact that I get to bring all my talents to the table and utilize them on a daily basis. I work well with a team or even on my own. I enjoy the freedom and responsibility that comes along with my position. The fact that I can see on a daily basis how my hard work pays off."

Most important skill or ability:

"For me that would be knowing the main points I need to address first, prioritize them, list them, and execute them. Organization would be the most important skill. As I mentioned before you do your daily graces and see where you are and where you need to go. I use my culinary education many times over and it is a plus for the principal to have a person like that. I enjoy organization and so do the people I have worked for. The ability to be organized and detailed in this field in paramount."

Favorite story:

"I was off and on one weekend when there was a builder driving in from out of town to pick up blueprints on a project. I made sure the principal knew all the details for this and that it was just a matter of greeting him, opening the door and giving him the plans. Simple enough. I was enjoying my day off spending time with friends when I received a call from the builder. 'I am here at the house ringing the bell with no answer.' I asked, 'Is the car in the driveway?' He said, 'Yes of course.' So I tried the house phone, the cell phone, and still no answer. I told him, 'Don't leave, I am on my way.' I arrived to the house one hour later and saw the cars in the drive way, I opened the door and announced my presence, went directly to the master room, knocked and knocked and said, 'I am here with the builder. If you are here, don't come out.' I did not know if anyone was home or not. I then heard a voice, 'Oh I forgot about that, thanks honey!'............ I said, 'You're welcome,' and just did what I had to do, no matter where I was or even if I was off. It's all about taking care of business."

Additional Private Service Profiles: Sean Sunkel, Estate Manager

Job Summary:

"I've been an Estate/Household Manager for multiple properties and homeowners in Connecticut and Colorado, including supervising support teams, coordinating construction and renovation crews, executing repairs personally, sourcing contractors for more elaborate projects, chauffeuring, and generally going above and beyond the call of duty to make my employers' lives easier. In short, I handle the details and deal with the problems, while they relax, spend time with family, travel, and enjoy themselves. My employers greatly appreciate my diverse skill sets in household management, staff management, event management, media production, technology implementation, real estate, and business/financial management. Homeowners have commented on my infallible work ethic and reliability in handling property- and staff-related matters promptly and discreetly. I'm used to being on call 24/7, serving as the point-person for crises and emergencies, and thinking three steps ahead of my employer to eliminate worry from their lives."

How I got started:

"I originally got started in my career twenty years ago as a top real estate listing agent in Ridgefield, Connecticut. At that time I carried a sizable inventory of homes that were on the market. Many of them required management in the owner's absence, which I provided. I started CastleGuard Estate Management in 2007 in response to requests from high-net-worth families looking for a trusted resource to manage their residences. I started out chauffeuring and helping with special projects primarily for three prominent families in Southeast Connecticut. Gradually my responsibilities increased for each of the families."

What I like most:

"One of the things I like most about my job is that it calls on all of my skills and experience; it is never boring. The most important skill or ability for me in this career is diversity. I am able to apply all of my diverse experience to Household Management including:

Household Management: Having worked for several families over the last six years, I am well prepared to serve on a full-time basis for one employer.

Real Estate Sales & Property Management: My real estate experience starting 20 years ago has given me an in depth understanding of all types of residential properties and the issues surrounding them. I am at ease with all aspects of real estate and large financial transactions.

Small business ownership/management: Over the last 8 years I have gained extensive experience in all aspects of household management, as well as staff management, payroll, administration, IT, bookkeeping, and facilities maintenance.

Event Management: Aside from being able to execute events of all sizes for my employers, I submit that household management and event management are very similar in many ways.

Technical: My years of audiovisual, video, and computer experience makes it easy for me to master advanced residential technical systems, and to provide support to those who use them.

Driving: It may sound basic, but professional driving involves a lot more than just getting from "point A" to "point B." My years of safe and reliable chauffeur experience are a valuable asset to my employers.

Sales: My sales experience gives me valuable negotiating skills and helps me present myself with poise and confidence.

Non-Profit Administration: As the Executive Director of a 501(c)(3) corporation in Aspen, Colorado, I became more skilled in the art of diplomacy, as well as organizational leadership and general management.

Entertainment: Performing in front of large audiences at an early age gave me a great deal of confidence in all aspects of my life going forward. More recent experience negotiating and booking well-known musical acts is an added benefit to my employers for their own entertainment needs."

Favorite story:

Over the past six years I have had the pleasure of providing a wide range of services for several Connecticut families. All of my employers have been a pleasure to work for, but one family stands out. I met Ken and Judith B. in early 2010 when they responded to an ad for my services. They were spending a good deal of time on the west coast and needed someone to manage their Connecticut home, as well as chauffeur them and help with various projects around the home. I worked for them on a part-time basis for three years during which time we developed a strong relationship of mutual respect and trust. Late in 2012 they decided to sell the Connecticut home and move to the west coast permanently. The home sold in April of 2013. Before they moved I asked if Ken could give me a letter of recommendation for my job search. The following is what Ken wrote:

'*We have had the pleasure and good fortune of knowing Sean Sunkel for over the past three years. In early 2010 we needed the services of someone to watch our home for extended periods due to frequent trips to California. We needed someone we could trust implicitly as well as be able to establish a comfort level in our dealings with this person. In our first meeting, Sean presented himself with confidence, knowledge of what was required and a list of references which clearly demonstrated his depth of experience. Over the past three years, Sean has fulfilled our wishes completely and far exceeded our expectations. He has directly handled issues such as extended power outages from hurricanes, severe snowstorms, heating and security system alerts. He has even searched for important documents in our files that we needed while away. Never did we once doubt that our home was in good hands. Our peace of mind from all of this was invaluable.*

Our standards of who we can trust are very high and Sean has truly exceeded that level in every way. We cannot say enough about his services or his character.

Kenneth B.'

Working in private service is rewarding in a number of ways. I get to meet interesting and highly successful people, I am constantly learning more about my profession, and I get paid well for my efforts. But Ken's letter of recommendation was one of my biggest rewards to date. I am excited about the future and I look forward to being of service for many more years."

Private Service Employment

Approaching the Private Service industry as a career takes careful consideration and a professional mindset just like any other career path. The most successful in our field often tell tales of finding service as a trade when they were young, and never leaving. It takes a certain mentality, attitude, and style to reach the highest levels of service positions, and we consider the private service model the pinnacle of service done right. Most of this guide is focused on those already exposed to the private service business, but some others successfully transition from related hospitality and management careers. Though it is extremely rare to find a high level private position without years of experience under your belt, if this seems like the path for you then get in touch with professionals in the field who might be helpful in guiding you along the way. Everyone's experience is different, but agencies mostly work with experienced candidates. Schools, personal referrals, and related temporary jobs may be avenues worth pursuing if you are just starting out. No matter what your stage of the game is, the following sections will apply to your efforts while seeking out the job you are after.

Finding a Private Service Position

When considering a career change, starting out in the domestic field, or finding your next position as a seasoned service pro, there are a few very important considerations. The first and most important is "Why do I want to work in private service?" Second, "What are my immediate and long-term goals in the industry?" And third, "How can I be competitive in the job search process?" Carefully and truthfully answering these questions will dictate how to proceed.

Why?

Many people looking for work in private service for the first time have an incomplete idea of the actual requirements for a position. Titles and job descriptions give some insight into the type of work expected, but the intangible and hidden details are where the true nature of the business is discovered. For example, can you honestly say that after years of building your own career and lifestyle that you now want to focus on the fulfillment of someone else? You need to understand that this is the one goal of service: to provide support for the employer above all. Are you capable of watching your boss spend more money in one day than you make in a year? You must have a disposition that allows for such dramatic realizations. Likewise, although several skills from the business world apply to domestic work, can you spot the little things that create harmony in a luxury lifestyle? Can you be a jack of all trades to assure things get done, no matter what? If so, you may be headed down the right path. If not, look for another direction with your career. The best way to know for sure if you are cut out to handle a domestic position is to ask a veteran. Get in touch with someone you may know in your personal network, or perhaps ask an agency or service association for a referral to a top candidate. You can likely find an event in your local area to attend and meet others already well-established in the field. Most people in the business are proud of what they do and are happy to give you some of their time. This is truly the only way to understand what happens on a day to day schedule, and the best way to know if it is for you.

For those already in the field, you still need to ask the hard questions of yourself. In my own experience I know I am no longer capable of private service as a profession. My years as a Personal Assistant were very dedicated and intensive as a 24/7 live-in employee. I can objectively review the efforts and sacrifices I made both physically and emotionally, and I feel like I've used up my ability to give that level of service in the employment arena. I could no longer be content or offer an employer my best while in the direct service role. I've considered it seriously over the years and know for sure that I could not be the best employee for the role. You need to assess this for yourself. If you are able to continue performing dedicated, personal service, or if you feel "born to serve," or perhaps like you have a "true service heart," then by all means, carry on. Likewise, if upon examination you find even a slight resentment, or a waning level of care for the service or principal, then look elsewhere. There are many other avenues of service oriented professions that may be rewarding for you, and there is no room for anyone bitter, resentful, or tired of high level private service. Remember always that personal service is not about you. You'll always want to establish a relationship that is equitable, but to be your best you will have to make it "all about them."

What?

What are your overall goals in the workplace for the next year? The next 3-5 years? The next 10 years? Do you have a plan that you are working toward such as owning your own business, retiring, going to school, etc.? If you know the answers here, you may be able use the domestic industry as your next stepping stone. For example, a domestic couple with some experience, excellent health, and flexibility with relocation can easily earn a salary of $80-120k and have all of their living expenses paid. With some planning and discipline, a 5-10 year stretch can put away enough money to meet some long term goals like starting a venture of your own or taking some time off. On the other hand, a position in private service does little to advance one's corporate career, so beware if that is a future goal. It is important to think a few steps ahead and look at your motivation when entering into or continuing a career in the private sector, because it is such a specialized and unique environment. Of course, if your true intention is to create a long-term career path within the industry, you are in the right place and the right frame of mind. If not, consider other options.

Another stumbling block in the job hunt is being able to prove your dedication. Newcomers and those returning to private service after a long time may find it hard to convince an employer that "this is what I really want to be doing." Similarly, providers who have been in business for themselves over a long period of time will need a great, convincing story about their return to singular employment. Have a very concise, carefully thought out answer to the question "Why do you want to do this type of work?" Using the specific duties of a position, match your reasons with skills and tasks you have been successful with or exposed to. You should give the impression that you know and can handle the upcoming job duties. In the same vein, having clear, positive reasons for moving forward from your last position is also essential. Framing your choice to find a new position or describing the reason your last role ended with positive statements and future goals is the mark of a service career pro. Either way, once you have it in your head and your heart that you want to do this type of work, it is time to begin searching.

How?

The most asked question of any agency is "How do I find a position?" First, if you made it to this point of the chapter and were honest with yourself all the way, step one, conviction, is complete. Step two is PREPARATION. If you do not read and understand the next chapter, "Becoming a Better Domestic Employment Candidate", you will not be ready to proceed. Before you go any further, you must have the specific tools to be successful. There is a list with detailed explanation in the chapter, so read it carefully and understand each item.

Step three is RESOURCES. Not everyone can do it alone. If you are reading this book, you probably are looking for some assistance in the search. Why not? It's mostly free and those who help you typically will benefit in some way. The following list includes the most likely targets for your job hunting effort.

Agencies:

Get on the phone and get on the internet to gather all the information you can stomach. Call agencies and ask for advice or referrals. Go through a few interview and application processes with them. Make sure to read and understand all the notes for "Working with Domestic Agencies" in this guide so you know the behind the scenes of what to expect. One of the best agency situations is a temporary agency. It will take some legwork to find one that has domestic or combination positions (domestic/executive), but this is one of the best ways to get experience with house management or personal assisting. For example, if you can get a job assisting a busy executive in their office, look for a situation where you can manage the personal duties as well. This includes gift buying, personal errands, pet care, scheduling and overseeing work at the residence, personal travel arrangements, etc. A fantastic resource is called The Job Seeker's Guide to Private Service Agencies, and is found at http://personaltouchcareerservices.com. A search through EstateJobs.com also offers profiles on many of the agencies posting jobs there.

Publications:

Although classifieds are one of the oldest ways to search, they are also one of the best. Often employers will try their own search before calling an agency and those willing to hire for a "starting" position probably won't use an agency. Check in the papers local to where you want to work and live. Another great feature of classifieds is that for a small fee you can place your own ad looking for the right employment situation.

Online:
Since our original guide came out in 2002 there has been exponential growth of online resources for job hunting. Industry specific job boards, agency online listings, and social media have become standard recruiting tools. Along with this relatively new arena come a number of pitfalls, so our advice is to tread carefully. You absolutely must be engaged with these resources in your job search, but you also must have a full understanding of what they can and can't do, and where you can go terribly wrong in your online activity. (More on this ahead...)

Networking:
If you are good with people, put the word out on the street about what you're looking for. Tell friends, relatives, former employers, etc. and start spreading the news. Most of the positions in the private service industry are filled this way. If you were looking for someone to work with your family and home, wouldn't you ask a trusted friend or associate? Of course you would. Just by getting your name in the right social circles you could end up with an amazing job. And perhaps a good showing will lead you to the next family on a referral from that one, and so on. Many long-time domestic professionals never go through a job hunt and frequently receive offers from friends of their employer. That is the level to aspire to.

Schools:
There are several schools to train you in private service. This is a path for the truly committed, so as before, step one (Conviction) is VERY important here. Schools are fairly expensive and do not guarantee placement upon graduation, but certainly the knowledge, experience, and dedication it takes to complete the courses is a step

in the right direction. Also, each school will have a placement service or leads for you to network for a job. (more resources!) Consult with the different programs out there to see if it makes sense for you based on your goals and your finances. Most of them can be found on the internet and you can also inquire through private service forums and social media.

Author's Note: There are currently several schools throughout The Americas, Europe, and other more remote locations. The main question we are asked about private service schools is "Are they worth it?" There is no short answer to the question, as every individual case needs to be considered in detail, but we have developed some very concise statements in response to those inquiries: 1. If you are enrolling in any educational program for the sole purpose of getting hired in a new job, DON'T DO IT. No matter what anyone says in their sales pitch, there are NO guarantees of employment upon graduation. . 2. If you have the time and money, take every course available! Career related education is a hallmark of professionals in any industry, and the quality of available private service education is, in my opinion, excellent. I have personally taken several wonderful courses through one institute, and was on the board of advisors for the curriculum at another great academy. I highly recommend continuing your education in your chosen profession at every opportunity.

In conclusion, a few basics are important to get a job in the private service field: Be sure of what you are after; be prepared for the opportunities; and use all available resources to give yourself a shot at the best possible employment.

Expert's View: Carol Scudere, Founder/Owner/Director, Professional Domestic Services and Institute

"The private service industry is unlike any other. It offers unique challenges and unique benefits. It is not a profession for everyone. It is one that requires a great attention to detail, a large amount of discretion, an ability to work in a fast-paced environment, and most importantly, a desire to provide the best service imaginable. The key to success in the private service industry is taking pride in going the extra mile for your employer. It is the responsibility of the household professionals to ensure that the home is a haven, a place for their employers to relax by themselves, with their family, and with their friends.

A service heart is crucial to excelling in the private service industry, but it alone is not enough. A private service professional must have the technical skills to clean a priceless work of art, hire contractors, manage a staff of many, prepare a travel itinerary, or coordinate several estates. Though, many entering the private service industry have experience managing their own household, managing another's home, especially one of wealth, comes with more responsibilities and more opportunities to make large, costly mistakes. As a result, receiving a proper education is one of the smartest things that aspiring and current private service professional can do. Attending a training program, such as Professional Domestic Institute's, can make a huge difference in an employee's likelihood of getting hired, their starting salary, their ultimate success, and the resulting raises and promotions.

The benefits of attending one of Professional Domestic Institute's several programs outweigh the time and financial costs. Training at Professional Domestic Institute, and other programs like it, equips its students with the knowledge they need to succeed. This is the primary reason that people seek training. However, the benefits go one step further. Seeking training says something about you as a person, something that is typically overlooked by students, but is obvious to employers. Getting your certificate in private service demonstrates to the employers that you are committed to the field and have worked hard to prove it. Actions always speak louder than words and the effort you put into their training will speak louder than anything you could write in a cover letter. With the knowledge acquired and the dedication demonstrated, training makes graduates stand out from the rest of the applicants, increasing the likelihood that they will get hired. In addition, at Professional Domestic Institute, every one of our students, who is in good standing, gets fully backed by our placement agency. Finding students a position is much easier than non-students because we simply know more about them. By attending a program, the placement officers know you personally and are able to market you more effectively and with greater confidence. With a reputable advocate that has experience with each student's strengths, weaknesses, desires, and needs, individuals who receive training have a better chance of not only landing a position, but landing a position that they love.

Furthermore, training allows employees to command a higher salary at their newly acquired positions. Many of our graduates can attest to this. One in particular, Veronica Davis, had been working as a housecleaner for many years. She attended our Estate Housekeeping program, and upon finishing, we landed her a position with a $15,000 increase in salary per year. That easily covered her cost of tuition within her first year. In addition, she was able to begin working for higher profile families because she now had the expertise they required.

Last but not least, training gives you the best chance at success in the private service industry. Learning while you go is not a strategy that works well when you are dealing with million dollars homes and the valuable, and often irreplaceable, items that make them up. Training will not only prepare you to complete all practical tasks immediately upon hire, but make sure you are aware of the expected attire, demeanor, and attitude expected of private service professionals. Your success as a household manager is dependent on the work that you do AND the way in which you carry yourself. Both of these things are not always intuitive, making training a critical step in ensuring your future growth in the industry. Once you have landed a position, the piece of paper you received is no longer helpful, but the knowledge that we impart makes all the difference.

One of our graduates, Sharon Larson, believes this wholeheartedly. She attributes all of her success in the industry to her training, her drive, and her commitment to go above and beyond for her employer. Sharon has worked with two high profile families in her 10 year career, through which she has been able to travel to Europe, shop with LA stylists, and meet former presidents. Her employers love her attention to detail, her ability to think ahead, and her organization, all things she claims are due to the wonderful and comprehensive education she received at Professional Domestic Institute. Sharon affirms, 'I don't know how people enter this industry without training. I can't imagine they are successful." She went on to talk about how in the past, she has looked at private service forums where people were discussing whether there is a need for training. She laughed saying, "People were saying that working as a household manager is commonsense, but it is not. Most people have $100,000- $200,000 homes. The people we work for have $10 million homes. It is night and day...You don't realize how important something like laundry is to these families. I work with $1,000 blouses. You can't just throw that in the laundry machine. You have to read the tag and talk to the dry cleaner. These are all things I learned from Carol.'"

When talking to Sharon, it also became very clear that an important part of training has nothing to do with technical tasks, but the role of the household manager in the family unit. Household managers become very close with their employers, which makes sense when you are involved with many personal matters. 'They often say that I am part of the family,' Sharon shares, "But I know that I am not and this is something that is very clear to me and was made very clear to me by Carol. They offer the use of their things, but I know that I cannot use them." Sharon understands that while it may feel like she is part of the family, there is strict boundary that would be unprofessional and inappropriate to cross. She recalls, 'I don't think that my employer knows anything about my personal life, nor should he.' One thing we try to cover in our training is that the employee-employer relationship is a one-way street, and if it becomes a two-way street, that is when the employers start to view you differently. They begin to not value you as the serious professional that household staff are finally being recognized as.

The private service industry has its perks, but those perks are earned by people who work long hours and have to occasionally do some undesirable tasks. However, one of the best things it offers is an outlet for the variety of skills that people pick up throughout their lives. Training allows people to build on their experience, as Veronica did with her cleaning skills. Or it allows new individuals to enter a field where they can apply their skills to a new and exciting career, as Sharon did. Sharon has her associates in Horticulture, which she uses to make floral arrangements. She has her Bachelors in Business Administration, which she uses to manage the budgeting. She used to work at dealership, giving her knowledge of high-end cars. By acquiring training, Sharon was able to translate all these things into the perfect career for her.

In the private service industry, you may start as just a household manager with only a couple of staff, or maybe none at all. But, once your employer realizes the extent of your expertise, your maturity, your dependability, and your discretion, it will not be long before you are solely responsible for the coordination of estates located in countries all over the world. This is a feat unlikely if you have not received a comprehensive and formal education at an established institution, like Professional Domestics Institute.

It may seem like a lot of money upfront to pay for a training program. However, it is an investment that will pay off in the long run. Sharon experienced this first hand. She was unemployed at the time of participating in Professional Domestic Institute's programs. She went into debt to finance her training and has never looked back. It has been a personal journey that she does not regret for a second. She remarks, "I have made 100 times what I paid for training, not including health benefits, bonuses, and the perks." But, she warns, "I definitely work a lot. It is a profession that is not for everyone."

Becoming a Better Employment Candidate

There are many approaches to finding employment as a domestic professional. You can respond to classifieds both on and offline, network through friends and former employers, or use a placement agency, to name just a few. No matter which path you follow to find a new job, there are some standard items that can help you rise above the other applicants in your field. Whether you are a Chef, Estate Manager, Chauffeur, Nanny, or any other type of employee, being prepared is the name of the game! It is also necessary to take a critical eye to the whole job search process and look at the specifics of your actions in each of the relationships of private service. You may be committing errors along the way that ruin your chances of moving forward. This section has a number of items for your job search overall, and the "Working with Domestic Employment Agencies" section contains notes regarding that particular relationship. Keep in mind that while these tips won't guarantee you get the job, messing up on some of them could eliminate you from a position that you otherwise might be the best candidate for!

Often in the private service industry, the candidates who get chosen in the early stages of the hiring process are not necessarily the ones with the most experience or the most skills, but those who understand basic business protocol in the job search. For example, a Chef may be extremely talented in his or her trade, but offer a very poorly written application package. He or she will stand less of a chance of getting an interview when competing against applicants with an up-to-date, well-constructed portfolio. (This actually seems to be more common among Chefs, being talented in artistic ways, and less focused on the resume presentation skills.) Likewise, should an agency or employer request background information or documents from a candidate, any delays could result in the hire of another applicant. In addition, if the information such as references, dates of employment, and contact numbers are hard to follow or incomplete, the application could seem "fishy" or the candidate could be thought of as incompetent.

For all of the above reasons, one should apply basic business "common sense" to the job hunt process. Spend some time educating yourself about conducting employment searches, interviewing, and writing a resume. Also, if you are planning to go through an agency for representation, the next Chapter, "Working with Domestic Employment Agencies," offers a behind-the-scenes perspective on the hiring procedure. Read carefully, because any inside knowledge and careful preparation will pay off tremendously as you go through the process of finding your next position.

In today's private service industry, there are a few specific items that will make you ready for any potential job opening. The list below is a great starting point for your job search process. By preparing all of the items, you will also become more clear in your own goals and choices for the employment you are seeking. For further tips on job hunting, visit sites online like monster.com and rileyguide.com (a personal favorite). Most of their advice and articles apply to all occupations and can be a great help. There's a tip I like to give before candidate go on interviews that also applies here. Do a web search for "Top 10 mistakes made on resumes" and you'll have enough material to be sure you don't mess up on obvious things. When interviewing, it's best to search for 'Top 10 interview mistakes."

As with any endeavor worth pursuing, the job search can be tedious and frustrating. Approach the task with a positive attitude and commit yourself to being ready for any obstacles along the way. Also "put your money where your mouth is" when creating your application materials. You may have to spend a few dollars to have a great look-ing resume package with clean, legible copies of all your documents (both black & white and color), but the payoff is far greater than the costs you will incur. Also with personal and community access to computers available almost anywhere, it is expected that all your ma-terials can be sent in a digital format and be edited as necessary. It is not acceptable for any top household employee to fax their hand written or hand notated resume to an agency or employer. Another common grievance is that agency applications are all different, te-dious, and ask for the same information as a resume. Well, too bad. If you can't give individual attention to the specific process that a company asks for, then don't work with them. You only hurt your-self by giving anyone a half-hearted effort in your job search. It may seem like lots of work on your part for little result, but that's what it takes. Hopefully you will only have to go through this once or twice in your lengthy career.

Overall, preparing carefully and placing yourself in front of all the opportunities available is the only way to get ahead of others com-peting for the same attention. If you are unsure of how to do any of the essential job seeker tasks then get an industry peer or ca-reer counselor to assist you. Here too the internet can be your best friend. There is a treasure trove of information available for free on sites like those mentioned above. Best of luck in your search!

Job Seeker Basics

At a minimum, anyone looking for a job in private service should have the following information on hand in both hard copy (printed documents) and available in digital copy for electronic distribution. As a side note, pay careful attention to document types and sizes for the ability to email and print files.

1. Current Resume

I cannot stress the importance of the resume enough. In many cases, it is the only item an employer will see when deciding on candidates to interview. Some agencies only send the applicant's resume to a client. Some employers only look at resumes and skip the rest of the pages. Make sure yours is up to date and has a professional look with no mistakes! You can hire a service if you are not good on the computer, and there are no excuses allowed for lack of computer skills or access to a computer. If you are not capable of this on your own, go immediately to your local library, community center, or job center and get yourself some computer training. It is unacceptable in 2013 to lack basic document preparation and online transfer skills. More details about specific formats and computer standards are ahead in this guide.

Expert's View: Donna Shannon, Personal Touch Career Services

Donna is one of the resume professionals we refer candidate to who need assistance with a strong private service resume. She has years of experience in the job search and resume environment and is particularly skilled in creating resumes for private service. We asked her to contribute some additional tips and details about resumes in our field.

"In a profession that requires attention to detail, a sense of aesthetics and a high level of expertise, your resume needs to reflect these same qualities.

Your resume should be a reflection of you on paper, especially in the private service industry. Employers and recruiters want to gain a sense of who you are before they pick up the phone. After all, they are trusting you with their most precious assets: their homes and their families. Your resume needs to be the first step in building that trust.

Resumes, biographies and portfolios for the domestic staffing and management industries are unique. Many of the so-called "resume rules" that apply for the business environment are not relevant to the luxury lifestyle management industry.

Did you know...?

Private employers will spend an enormous amount of time reading your resume:

Business resumes only have to stand up to a 30 second reading. While a private employer may gain an impression of your resume in 30 seconds, it is not uncommon for them to pore through each and every detail.

Recruiters are frequently asked for more details about the candidate's skills, abilities and experience long before the actual phone interview is scheduled. With a detailed resume, candidates and recruiters alike are more comfortable answering these in-depth questions - which helps job seekers get hired faster.

Staffing agencies do not have enough time to re-write your resume:

They need to spend their time with their clients - the employers - in order to find and fill job openings. Your resume is your responsibility - even if an agency puts it in their own format.

It is not uncommon for a recruiter or placement agency to copy-and-paste information from a candidate's resume into their own format for branding purposes. This, however, is NOT the same as re-writing the content. Recruiters prefer to have a highly detailed resume from the candidates. It is always easier to trim a resume down to meet their purposes than to create content from a bare-bones resume.

Not only that, a polished resume will speed up the recruiting process. Placement agencies are under pressure to turn around candidates quickly when the right job appears. If your resume is easy to work with, comprehensive, detailed and polished, it is more likely to be presented to an employer.

A private service resume can be significantly longer than a traditional one-page resume:

A typical business resume is 1-2 pages. In private service, all of your talents and skills are relevant for your resume. Because lifestyle management careers take into account all of your abilities - including your hobbies, personal experiences and natural talents - it often takes 2-4 pages to convey enough information for the potential employer to appreciate everything you can do for him or her.

For the experienced Manager, it is necessary to show expertise in ALL of the major functions of an estate. This could be everything from managing the multi-million dollar renovation to planning a child's birthday party, from taking the cat to the vet to coordinating travel with the private jet. To capture all of your experience, the resume must be flexible enough to reflect all of your diverse talents.

Private service resumes may cover your entire career:

Business resumes focus on only the past 10-15 years. Since all of your skills can work in a household position, employers want to see everything you've done - which can span 20-30 years.

These are just a few examples of how the typical "rules for resumes" don't apply to the private service professional! However, changes in recent years have forced an evolution for private service resumes....

The Corporate Influence

As more of the principals' family offices or HR departments becomes involved in the hiring process, domestic management resumes need to adapt. As such, your resume should adopt some of the corporate tactics. Try these three tricks to catch the interest of the screeners:

1. Concise Profile Section

Previously, the Profile section might have included where the candidate grew up, number of siblings, religious affiliation, marital status and other very personal details. This kind of disclosure can make HR people very uncomfortable; legally, they can't ask these kinds of things and don't understand why you're saying this stuff.

What they really want to know is why someone would want to do this job. Not everyone understands a passion for service, and making a strong statement about the personal satisfaction is a powerful tactic. Next, they want to know the candidate's work style. Is he reserved, or is he more extroverted? Is she a strong leader who can take direction? They may include where they grew up here, but make sure it relates to the work style. For example, a Brooklyn native has a very different style than a PA from Los Angeles.

There are times when a potential employer will want a complete biography. In this case, make it a stand-alone document, not part of the resume.

2. Key Word Optimized (KWO) Skill Set

Many people are familiar with the term SEO, or "Search Engine Optimized." For websites, these are the key words and phrases that are imbedded into the website to generate search engine traffic. Resumes work much the same way - recruiters and HR professionals rely on specific key words to find the right people for their open positions.

When HR uses an Applicant Tracking System (ATS), or online application process, having the right key words becomes even more important. Why? Because a computer program is screening the candidates, often removing more than 50% of the field before a human being sees a single resume.

Without the right key words, your resume will never be found. Worse, lacking the right key words in your LinkedIn profile will cost you additional opportunities as more recruiters rely on social media to find both active and passive candidates.

Solid skills such as "management of up to 10 staff members, event planning for 100 guests and gourmet-quality chef" belong in a bulleted skill set section, usually on the first page of your resume. This helps both the screeners and the principals appreciate your value right away.

Be sure to include your computer skills as well. As domestic management has evolved, solid computer skills are more important than ever. State all of your abilities by software/hardware name and proficiency level.

Professional Associations

Including your professional associations is very important on the resume, especially with more corporate recruiters getting involved in private staffing. As mentioned, HR won't understand our industry. Showing involvement with an association gives credibility to private service as a whole. Remember to list the organization out by full name, not just acronyms, along with the website."

2. Letters of Recommendation

Any time you leave a job you should get a letter of recommendation. Try to have them written on company letterhead or personal stationery of your employer. The more letters you have, the better. Be prepared to distribute copies that are as clear as possible. Even better, have color copies made of the most recent or most important letters, and like the resume, have scanned, clear, reasonably sized computer versions available for sending. This particular aspect has a few nuances to be aware of. The privacy concerns and confidentiality issues apply when sending out employer names, addresses, and contact information. Before submitting these elements make sure you understand what a company or individual is doing with the information and what their reference verification process is. Sometimes it is appropriate to have "privatized" versions of your recommendations with names and contact information blacked out for security.

3. Reference List

You will have to supply this information on any job application so have it ready on a separate page, laid out as follows: Employer name; whom to contact for the reference; the contact's title; a current telephone number; and any notes about reaching the person. You may also request to be contacted directly for telephone numbers so you can tell your reference in advance who will be calling. Like the reference letters, this is the most sensitive information you will be disclosing. At a professional, top level in the field, we will respect a candidate's request to hold reference checking until there is a pending job offer. This arrangement is on a person by person basis, so communicate clearly with the agent if you need to maintain a high level of confidentiality. It is not a good idea to send this information to an online job application without first knowing and contacting the representative for the client.

Author's Note: It is painful to admit how many job seekers will not provide basic reference information for their past employment. In our role as employment agents, references will often determine if we can even work with an applicant. There are several nuances to the reference game, but the basics are unchanging. We need to verify where you worked, when, and how your employer felt about your performance of the job. If we can't do this, we can't help you, period.

4. Current Photograph

We sometimes get questions about this from a legal or discrimination angle. It is not within our scope of expertise to give legal advice here, but let's just say that if you are concerned about showing someone a photo of yourself as a professional employment candidate, you may be in the wrong career. Most, if not all, employers will be critical of the physical appearance of their staff. In addition to providing the service flow of a home, the staff in the "front of house" represents an aesthetic consistent with the employer's taste and image. Therefore the physical aspect of "fit" in a private home becomes important depending on your place in the service structure. Of course this will vary from job to job, but let it be said that our clients are more than likely to differentiate two equally skilled candidates based on their professional appearance.

That said, have a recent photograph of yourself ready to give out (color photocopies are a good idea) with an application, in addition to a digital copy for emailing, etc. It should show your overall physical appearance with a clear shot of your face. Another nice touch is to be in the uniform of your profession. (For example, a Chef can include a photo of them in action in a working kitchen.) In most cases an agent or employer that you cannot visit locally will want to see your overall physical presentation, just as they would in a face-to-face interview. Though not the same, a quality photograph is an excellent opportunity to show yourself positively. You can stage the picture in your best professional dress with appropriate grooming for the position you seek and offer this as your interview presence when only a telephone meeting is available. Today's technology is also moving the recruiting industry toward video interviews and profiles. If you are comfortable with it, a video introduction is an amazing way to showcase your physical, professional presence and communication skills. It is like having a first interview before any candidates are even chosen.

5. ID
Usually agencies will ask for your identifying documents upfront to verify you are who you say. This includes driver's license, social security card, passport, green card, work visa, etc. Requirements vary for interviews with agencies and employers, but without exception make sure you have ample identification to prove your identity and the required employment authorization of the job. If you have any questions about acceptable documents, you MUST ask in advance what you will need. The best guidelines for standard employment authorization are found in the US government's I-9 form. http://www.uscis.gov/files/form/i-9.pdf

6. List of Previous Addresses
To conduct background checks, employers or agencies will require a list of the county, city, state, and address of where you have lived over the past 10 years. Have this information available and typed out. Make copies. This is the standard for any reputable background screening company. Sadly most in-depth searches are still performed by hand and this county-by-county listing will guide a thorough background report process.

7. Background Explanation
If there is anything derogatory at all that you know will show up on your: driving record; credit history; criminal background; or any civil litigation cases, have a detailed explanation ready. When these checks are done on you, the reports come back with codes and sketchy details about the events that are difficult to interpret. Your willing discussion of the incident can make certain situations less

incriminating as a candidate for employment. Treatment of background information has come under much scrutiny lately, especially in California. There are certain conditions where applicants cannot be chosen based on information in their consumer credit file. You can check with state laws if there is some concern about this. That said, most private employers either don't fall under the rules or don't follow them. When the security and wellbeing of their families are at stake you can bet they will want to look at any potentially relevant "skeletons" in an employee's closet. Ideally the best employees in private service will be quite boring people, having nothing in their histories to even consider. However, there are some exceptions and easily explained circumstances that come up in public record. The perfect scenario is to have nothing on file whatsoever, with a close second being simple entries that can be quickly identified and justified.

Interviewing: Remember the Premise

There are far too many nuances and better sources to learn about specific interviewing techniques than we can present here. For that reason we'll just focus on the interview as part of the search process and consider how you should approach it. The way you think about interviewing in general will affect everything you do along the way. The biggest mistake we find with candidates in the interview stage (with agencies and employers) is forgetting the reason, or premise, of the job search. You must remember, without exception, that your goal is singular: To obtain the job offer. Focusing on this desired result will help you frame all interactions and efforts in your job search, relationships with agencies, and protocol with current and past employers. It can also help you stand out as the better employment candidate, appearing more professional and service oriented than your competition.

Let's start with the top three problems that arise when job seekers forget they are aiming for the offer, *every time*. The first and most obvious issue to employers is a lack of interest or enthusiasm. The attitude you show toward any position, even if it does not seem like a perfect match for you, is critical. Any hint of boredom or doubt about the situation offered is immediately picked up and considered a reason to eliminate you. This is so subtle, yet we've seen it ruin top employee's chances at great jobs again and again. A client will call back and tell us, "They didn't seem interested in the job." (I actually lost my first amazing job offer out of college for this exact reason, and never forgot it!) Don't ever let this be the reason you lose the offer. The second, similar offense is being too direct and confrontational about job details at an early stage. Sometimes the client is developing the job and ready to make adjustments for the right employee. You must allow for this possibility. We've even seen entirely new roles formed for the "right" candidate who interviewed for something else! Don't hammer away during the early interviews about specific schedules, compensation details, future prospects for the position, etc. Starting with any hint of "It's all about me" mentality knocks you out of the running almost automatically. I'm not suggesting here that you should move blindly into any interview or position, but these tips are for the professional who can use an expert approach to let the details unfold toward the job offer. Trust me, once you are the target candidate for the employer, everything can be worked out and all details made appropriately clear. The third type of mistake is the proverbial "burning bridges." Whatever you do, consider each professional contact as having the potential to enhance your career. Private service is a small niche and word will always get around when you are rude, offensive, loose with your information, or make another similar misstep. If you can't maintain professional composure in the face of difficult people and frustrating activities, then you are certainly in the wrong line of work.

So how do we take these mistakes and turn them positive? By returning to the main premise and filtering all your activity through that lens. Be the best candidate from start to finish, and get the offer. One of the most important and effective ways to implement this filter is to reframe all of your questions as beneficial to the employer. Let's say you want to find out the schedule details during an interview with the employer. Instead of "How many hours will I have to work in an average week?" try offering, "What would you consider the ideal schedule to make this role effective for your household?" Or "What hours of service in this role would best accommodate your personal schedule?" There are infinite variations of the same language, but the point is to always be referencing your service to the employer as a benefit. Another example can be used to inquire about the future of the position. Asking an employer "How do you see this role continuing to add value to your home in the future? Are there other goals you have in mind for this person's contribution a few years from now?" Again, a small change in language changes the meaning and tone so significantly that it could change the outcome of the interview. Do some research on your own for asking appropriate interview questions, and discuss or practice with a colleague. This can seriously make or break your chances at an offer.

Another very important way to implement your "Get the Offer" premise is in relationship. Have basic protocol throughout your interview steps, including thank you notes, timely follow up with agents and employers as directed, and an overall positive attitude toward any position. Remember, if you come out of an interview and spew all the negatives to your agency, their obligation to the client is to eliminate you! If there are questions or doubts, consider moving forward with polite, professional discussion about further details at the appropriate time. The last thing you want to do is eliminate yourself by making assumptions or letting little things ruin the overall job prospect. Make sure you know definitively that the job is not for you before you choose to complain or decline. If you are working through an agency, they will assist you in the discovery process along the way. But remember, for everyone's benefit, be the best candidate possible until you reach a point that you can make an informed decision. Unfortunately we can't teach attitude. This is perhaps the one area where you will have to make a simple choice for yourself, and play the part as necessary. If you really need to "fake it" day in and day out, and have no sincere enthusiasm for a service role, find a new career.

The same idea applies to engaging former, current, and future employers. In all circumstances, choose the most gracious and accommodating path for the employer's sake. For instance, giving proper notice when ending a position, offering to rearrange a vacation to do a trial interview or start a new job early, speaking in a complimentary way about past employment even if it was a living hell, etc. can all go a very long way in how you are viewed during your career. The opposite behavior would be shown in suing an employer over minor discrepancies, speaking poorly of past jobs, telling potential new employers about your own needs before you are their top candidate, quitting and leaving a job out of anger or to prove a point, etc. You are not in this business to change anyone, so vendettas and ill will have no place in your attitude or actions during the interview and employment phase. Be aware if you are making these mistakes and correct your course to a positive one. As rapper Ice Cube famously stated, "You better check yourself before you wreck yourself."

Author's note: Sometimes a candidate will end up with multiple interviews during their job search. Inevitably it seems that if a job offer comes through, another interview will be still in progress and the job seeker does not know what to do. The advice I've been giving for years is this: Consider the actual job offer, regardless of any other potential offer or upcoming opportunity, and make a yes or no decision. Period. The end. Final answer. If it is the right job for you, accept it and graciously inform all other parties that you have taken a new position. Though this may be disappointing to others (agency or employer) they will understand completely. Give your 100% focus and effort to the new position and employer, and congratulations! On the other hand, if it is not the job for you, don't take it just because you need a job and will continue looking for the next best thing. This is a disservice to everyone. Politely decline and move on. The only exception to the rule is when there are existing arrangements for a trip to an interview. You should fulfill the obligation to the interviewing family. Inform the family or agent who gave you the job offer that you need just a few days to give them a final answer due to a prior interview arrangement. Make sure you maintain your complete enthusiasm for the offer, just let them know that out of professional consideration for the other family and/or agency you need to complete the other interview. Yes, they too will understand.

Principals with Principles – Job Search Standards and Errors

Nobody's perfect, as the saying goes, but if you are presenting yourself as one of the highest level service providers in the world, you had better be close! Over the years we have seen so many blatant errors, mistakes, and outright screw-ups on resumes of those purporting to be experts in their field that it has become embarrassing. When trying to represent a profession as having equal merit to other careers, there is a certain level of basic knowledge and attention to detail that needs to be demonstrated. All too often we see the opposite, including an ironic favorite scenario of job applicants stressing their "exacting standards," or "attention to detail," only to find a spelling or grammar error in the next sentence. In lighter instances we see a few typos, grammar mistakes, and common misspellings. In the more serious offenses we have applicants who misspell their own names. (No, I'm not kidding, and it happens regularly!) For this reason we are dedicating an entire section to the errors candidates are making in their job search paperwork. What follows is a sampling of items that we have either experienced or continue to be surprised by when working with job seekers across the country. Remember, for most of you these will be simple reminders, but for many a thorough review and consideration is warranted.

Author's Note: Throughout my writing here and in the daily agency operation, I too will fall short in some of the areas discussed. I ask for your exemption in this case, however, while I am functioning as a "coach" and attempting to present the ideal standards to follow for your success. Certainly we all make mistakes, but in the role you are playing as an applicant there is very little tolerance under the critical eye of employers and agents in private service.

Writing, Language, and Terminology

Misuse of common terms in our business is one of the most serious and most overlooked issues we see time and time again. As the section heading indicates, there are two completely different spellings and meanings for the word pronounced [prin-suh-puhl]. If there was one term I could eliminate from the private service jargon that would be it. So let's clear it up here and now: If you are referring to the owners of the home in which you work, they are PRINCIPALS. If you are having trouble with unscrupulous employers, then you are questioning their basic PRINCIPLES. Anyone reading this guide who submits these terms in error will find me not so friendly in the future. This is a serious pet peeve because it represents very important terminology for our business and those who misuse the word are guilty of either lying about their knowledge in private service or just don't care to proof their work. PLEASE get this straight.

Another term that really misses the mark is "State Manager." I'm certainly open to being wrong about this one, but I have never been able to find, even in foreign language translations, a position within private service by this title. If you are attempting to use this term to mean Estate Manager, you probably don't have the right description for your role. Please pay careful attention to this "overlay" technique where you are awarding yourself a formal title in retrospect. If you were truly hired in a role that had the title of Estate Manager, there would be no confusion on the use and/or meaning of the words. If you are trying to use a title to describe the functions of your previously untitled role, please select one of the titles you understand completely, and use it correctly. Titles do vary as we discussed earlier, but slight differences in duties are not what we are talking about here. We can tell a great deal about a candidate's level of industry knowledge by how they use titles in their resume, and how they ultimately explain the roles in an interview.

Some of the more offensive mistakes include misspelling of employers' names, agent names, and just about every proper noun in a resume. Don't overlook these errors. Your resume can be in the trash because of a simple typo. And a personal favorite of mine, if only for the humor, is never abbreviate the word Assistant as "Ass." It's certainly good for a laugh, but it's also good for making you look bad. Here are a few tips from the most common (and sometimes comical) errors and oversights we notice.

File Names

This one is so subtle, but so egregious when messed up. The naming of electronic documents when sending files is very important. Silly, overly lengthy, or inappropriate filenames are a negative you want to avoid. For example, naming a resume "agencytemplate2010.doc" can indicate carelessness or lack of effort. Similarly, a filename like "jackmillerresume_secondedit_foragencies_december2013.PDF" is simply too long and cumbersome in most file systems. Technically this is significant as well, as the wrong filename extension can load the wrong program on the viewer's device.

Document Templates

If you use a template for a cover letter or resume, make sure to fill out all fields appropriately and clear those not in use. Don't ever send out a document that includes "Type Name Here" or "Enter Date" kinds of text still on the page. You might even consider checking authoring and editing information to make sure you are listed as the document author, even when you have editing help.

Contact Notes

If you really want to waste someone's time, call them with an incorrect reference to vague information that you can't remember the source of. I say that quite facetiously because at least a few times each week we handle such a call. We'll be asked about a job or an application that didn't come from us or any of our resources, and when questioned for the source the job seeker replies, "Oh, I'm sorry, I've just applied to so many of these things. I can't keep it all straight." If that's the case, we can't help you. Treat your job search like an employer's travel plans and insurance documents. Know whom you are calling, what it is about, and relevant notes or history related to the matter. Otherwise, don't call. Your job search is your responsibility so keep the information organized and filed appropriately.

Email Addresses and Usernames

Your email address and some of your usernames and passwords may be visible to the company you are applying with. Make sure you aren't using crazy, silly, or too personal names in these fields. (More on this ahead.)

Poor Translation

Regardless of your native language, your resume should have no mistakes in the language you write it in. You must have someone with excellent language and grammar skills review your resume if it is not penned in your first language. No exceptions.

Telephone

The telephone is your friend. Don't betray your friend. In our era of modern technology we seem to have forgotten the virtues of making a simple phone call. This may not be the case with everyone in the business, but in our office we appreciate receiving phone calls. Good phone manners and the personal connection of a conversation are very, very welcomed. The main idea is to be professional, respectful, and helpful for making successful connections in the employment relationship. But be warned! In the same way that a phone call can be give the best impression, any telephone mistakes can offer an equally poor impression. Here are some notes on making the right connection:

Voicemail

If you have a primary telephone number on your resume with no voicemail or answering machine, good luck! There are very few in the business who will try to call someone back who does not answer the phone. This goes also for call waiting. If the line does not roll over to voicemail when you are on the phone, you WILL miss important calls. On the same note, make sure you have call waiting, because there is no tolerance for a busy signal these days. It is also crucial to have a respectable outgoing message on your machine or voicemail service. Please don't have a recording of your kids' first words and laughing fits. Identify yourself clearly and be brief. Nobody has patience to wait through a message that is too cute or too long when all they want to do is leave you a message to call back! In the other direction, when you receive a voicemail make sure you listen to it. Don't press the call-back button in a frenzy because you missed an important call. Take a moment to make sure whether or not a message was left by the caller. If yes, then listen to it before returning the call. There may be an alternate number or other call-back instructions left, or there may be a question that you need to gather information for. This goes along nicely with the overall rules for being prepared when making any phone calls related to your job search.

Multiple Phone Numbers

Here's another technology that has been turned on its head over the last few years. There used to be a simple expectation of making a phone call to one number and either having the person answer, or having a machine take a message. Now we have cell phones, land lines, work numbers, Skype and internet phones, etc. Though convenient in some ways, the ability to reach a person directly is greatly diminished. While it is acceptable to give both your home phone and cell phone for the caller to choose, we prefer one definitive point of contact. If you can indicate or simply use the one best number that you will either answer or receive messages on, that is very helpful. In addition to being reached, other tangles arise from multiple phone locations. For example, if you give a work number on your resume it could create some very awkward situations on the job. Your best practice here is to use one main number for contact, be sure to have voicemail in place, and answer if you are able.

Basic Etiquette

Please be sure all pets and children are attended to when you make a call. Though we understand parenting responsibilities, there is nothing worse than a shrieking child or incessantly barking dog on the phone with you. Some will overlook this, but in general it is not going to leave a good impression. Likewise, there is no excuse for ever eating, drinking, smoking, loud gum chewing, or other functions taking place during a call. This is so simple, yet violated by so many. The bottom line is "Think before you call." Another pet peeve is when someone calls several times in a row, hoping that we will pick up. Many times you are calling a small office or an individual who is likely on the other line. If you don't get an answer on the first try, leave a message. We all have voicemail for a reason. Please use it politely. This even applies when the office is closed, because we'll notice the caller ID coming up a number of times consecutively. Be patient. You can always follow up if someone has not returned your call within a reasonable time frame. (Usually 2-3 business days.)

Caller ID

This is something often overlooked because only the call recipient sees the result. If you are calling from someone else's phone or a location where you don't want to receive a return call, make sure you tell us. Another option is to block caller ID before making the call. What these both prevent is having someone call you back by redialing and reaching the wrong number. Also, don't call from confidential numbers! You would be surprised how many confidential employers have caller ID that easily identifies them personally or through their company. Overall, make sure you know the outgoing caller ID of the line you are using, and if you are not certain that it will be appropriate, then block the service before dialing.

Mobile Phones

When you give out your cell phone as a primary contact number there is an inherent expectation of reaching you quickly. Answer the phone if you can at all times during a job search, and if your conversation will be compromised in any way, suggest returning the call as soon as you are able to speak without distraction. This can include bad reception, other people nearby, background noise, while dining, when driving, etc. Remember that as convenient as mobile phones are, they still really stink for voice clarity and coverage. If you can avoid doing business on the mobile, great. Call back on a land line or in a quiet location where and when you have excellent reception. A few general tips for mobile phone protocol that need professional consideration are:

If your time window to finish a conversation is too tight, it is your responsibility to suggest calling back later or scheduling a time to speak.

Answer the phone properly and politely ALWAYS. I can't stress this enough. If you are in the middle of a job search and might receive an important call, don't act like an insurance salesman is calling. Being rude or angry is the absolute worst first impression we can have in reaching out to you. I've eliminated candidates based on this alone, within the first five seconds of speaking with them. There is no need to be nasty, ever, and especially if your phone number is out on resumes to potential employers.

Don't answer if you can't talk. Second only to being rude is the scenario when a phone is answered only to here "Who is this?...Oh, I'm sorry I'm driving and eating a donut and getting a massage so call me back!" Of course I am exaggerating here, but in any similar situation, if you can't physically complete the call, don't pick up!

Please don't call in or expect to have any length of conversation while driving. It is unreliable, distracting, and annoying. If driving is your only window of time to make the call, then carefully consider obstacles, distractions, dead zones, parking garages, etc.

Surprisingly, many job seekers do not pay attention to which time zone they are calling. National and international locations for agencies and employers are very common, so make sure you know what time you are trying to reach someone.

Never have a friend, spouse, sibling, or other person call on your behalf. If we need to correspond with you, we want to speak directly to you. Unless there is an emergency or you physically can't be reached for a period of time, call for yourself. Don't have others attempt do your work.

When using a cell phone and leaving a voicemail, assume you have a bad connection and speak clearly and slowly. You should also repeat any numbers, emails, times, directions, or any important data.

Email

Email is not the same as texting your friends. To be safe, you should treat emails as business letters and documents. Remember that all forms of written correspondence are examples of your work, even when casual language is used. Be professional in all your writing throughout the job search process. You never know what samples may be in front of an agent or potential employer! Common email mistakes include:

Silly Email Names

This one should be simple, but you would be surprised how many people send silly email addresses in professional documents. If you have an email that sounds unprofessional in any way (ask a friend for an opinion) then get yourself a new, free email address for work related connections. Likewise, any names that sound sexually suggestive, or otherwise don't belong in a board room, should be eschewed in favor of a simple, new address.

Group Emails

Please, do not send group emails or spam or forwards to an agent or employer. If you have any of the above on a group list, please delete now! All emails should have a direct purpose for specific people. General emails are rarely replied to, and most importantly, if we have any reason to block your email address (because of spam or sending irrelevant items) your future interaction with us will be severely hampered. The other technical error under the same heading is using auto-responders. We recommend having a separate email for use in your job search if necessary so any employment contacts can get to you without restrictions. Even if you are truly "out of the office" at your current job, or on vacation in Tahiti, let all job related information reach you at an appropriate address.

Email Permissions and Spam Filters

Many times when you work with an agency they will include you on an update list for job listings and important announcements. Make sure you pay attention to what you have signed up for and allowed on your end. It is important to let desired emails come through and not miss notes from people relevant to your job search. You might choose to set your email service to allow messages from the domains where you sign up for jobs. Likewise, your emails may be filtered when sending resumes and attachments to an agency or private employer so it is a good idea to follow up after a few days to make sure your items were received.

Missing Information

On many occasions we will receive emails with either no name, or simply a first name as your closing signature. Unless we immediately recognize your email address or you are replying in a conversation already started, this is a big problem. You might not get a reply. Please use your full name and email address in every conversation via email. It is also a good idea to add your phone number to emails, in case your contact is pulling up the email on a mobile device, or wants to call you immediately while reading your note. This goes for every type of contact, including phone messages. Be sure to identify yourself and provide information to reach you directly.

Too Much Information (TMI)

Email signatures are great for sending contact data with your communications. However, in a professional setting, the signature field should never be used to promote or express any of your outside interests or preferred sayings, quotes, beliefs, etc. Again, considering your audience, you never know if the reader of your quote will have alternative views, and dismiss you for something that simple! It is far better to keep those ideas out of all business writing.

Another very serious error under TMI is committed when you send job search emails from your current employer's email. There are nearly permanent records of everything that is sent online, and it also violates many non-disclosure promises to send around your employers' email data. This goes for faxing as well. The headers and information contained in both faxes and emails should be kept confidential for the benefit of your employers. Be smart about where you are sending from and where you choose to receive email and faxes during a job search.

A final note on emails is that when you send is also important. If you send emails at 2 am or other strange hours relative to the time zone, it will either look strange to the recipient or possible get filtered by spam programs. If that happens to be the real hour that you work best, set a delayed send or wait to send your message during more reasonable hours. Of course this tip is not a "do or die" issue, but highly recommended. Never forget, we are trying to appear as professional as possible and give no reasons for being excluded as a candidate.

Technology and Social Media

Instant Messaging

Unless an agency or employer requests that you "ping" them through an instant message service, don't do it. Your message asking for them to join you online or let your message through will be denied or ignored. The same goes for Skype or other online services with a chat style option. Just because you may have connected on a prior login for an interview, it does not mean you can continue to chat directly at any time. Be sure which communication methods are accepted and permissible in general before reaching out at random.

Personal Websites and Online Profiles

It goes without saying that whatever you choose to post online should be considered public information. The only way to be sure nobody will see an online item is to never post it in the first place. I won't preach too much here, but it must be said that your online image is now and forever part of your overall resume profile. Agencies and employers WILL search online for anything they can find about you, so you had better know exactly what is going to be visible. I like to say that "Full disclosure is the new privacy." What I mean is that no matter what people see online about you, they should come away completely unaffected and slightly bored. If you have nothing at all to hide and can maintain a "saintly" appearance, then go ahead and post all you want. But be warned, anything that could distract or give a wrong character impression during your job search can and will hurt you.

Facebook

I really enjoy connecting with friends and family on the world's social supersite. I made a decision several years ago to keep all of my connections as private as the site's settings will allow, and only connect with non-business related contacts. (On my personal profile) Even though I am very skilled at online navigation and privacy matters, I still choose not to post anything too controversial or out of character that could be taken the wrong way. It just does not bode well for maintaining a professional appearance, and that applies even more while job hunting. If you have something important to share that is a bit racy or could anger others, save it for direct messaging or conversation. You just don't need to take the risk.

LinkedIn

LinkedIn makes it very easy to connect in good business form. You can actually use this site to your networking and online profile advantage. We recommend creating a very detailed profile of yourself and your professional experience. This is a great way to reach out to others in the same field and look for potential connections. The one HUGE pitfall of the site regards employer privacy and discretion. Even if you have permission to list your past employers on your resume, posting to a public forum with their names open to anyone is not a good practice. Save sensitive information exclusively for the application and interview process.

Personal Websites

If you are good with web creation and basic layout, creating a personal website is an excellent idea. The basic idea is to have a complete profile of yourself on a cloud based location that you can direct the appropriate audience to. You can showcase any information (discreetly, of course) about your skills and experience, as well as uploading multiple photos and even videos of yourself in action. The multimedia experience is becoming both simpler and more widely accepted as a way to distribute your information in a job search. Other possibilities include storage space and website sections that you can make private for sharing with friends and family. This is by far the most secure way to handle anything personal online.

Author's Note: Many businesses use Microsoft's Outlook for their email and organizational tasks. (We do.) There is a new feature (since the 2010 version) called Outlook Social Connector that many people are not familiar with even though it is having a major impact on social media and business. Anytime we receive an email or have contact with our known lists of candidates, there is a section of the screen that displays your latest information on Facebook, LinkedIn, and other social sites. This works automatically, without your involvement, for any information that you have not shielded with privacy settings! So sending a resume now might also mean showing us your Facebook profile photo and the latest cute kitten video you shared yesterday. Get educated right away with these programs and settings! We highly recommend an associate of ours for Microsoft training and related social media elements: Company Founder, Microsoft Productivity Instructor/Presenter & Bestselling Author Vicki Sokol Evans. Her fantastic classes and training information may be found at http://www.redcapeco.com. This will also be a very pertinent security issue when working with a staff at any employer's residence or company. You MUST know what information is being shared when you have distinct privacy concerns.

As a final note on social media and online profiles, make sure any use of these elements provides consistency and not confusion. Many times we'll review a professional service resume with a very focused career path, then see the same person listed in an entirely different line of work on LinkedIn! This can be really conflicting for an agent or employer looking at your overall work profile. Are you a House Manager, or a Real Estate Agent? A Personal Assistant, or general contractor? It is easy to understand the different uses of your online persona, but when searching for a job, less is more!

Job Boards

If there is one online item that has most impacted the job search, the job board is it. Though fairly new in the history of technology, there is nothing at all new about the Help Wanted ads! Online job searching is no more complex than sifting through newspaper ads of old, as long as you have a grasp of the technical side of this new, essential job search tool. The first and last rule to solve 99.9% of any problem you will encounter in job site use is very simply: *Read everything carefully*! I'll admit I'm as guilty as the next person when it comes to skipping "terms of service" agreements and agreeing to use everyday sites like Amazon and ebay. But when it comes to something as important as finding employment and transferring sensitive information online, you had better take a moment and consider the weight of your actions. That said, most sites will have very explicit directions, a help section, a phone number to call for help, or all of the above. Use them all. If you don't have a complete understanding of what you are doing online with your job search, always favor taking your time to get it right versus submitting the wrong thing quickly.

The second thing to comprehend about the online job board is that there are very few standards for what to expect in return for your efforts. I wish I could snap my fingers and make this one different. Running EstateJobs.com allows us to have elaborate feedback about agency and job hunting experiences, and the range couldn't be greater. Some agencies will not respond to an application unless you are a perfect match and they want to speak with you about a particular job. Others will set up auto responders to let you know they received an email from you. We happen to reply to every application on our job boards, even if we use Craigslist for an ad. I think it is a great standard, though it proves incredibly difficult at times. The sheer volume of responses can be overwhelming on job listings. Our advice here is very simple. Use the job sites as one tool in your search, maintain your own professional conduct, and follow up appropriately if you can. Other than that, try not to get frustrated. I assure you that if you are a great fit for a job (from the employer's perspective) then you will get a response. Some job seekers have suggested that agencies post "fake" ads to draw in more resumes. This is rarely true or even possible based on the amount of work involved. Sometimes ads are left posted after being filled in case a placement does not work out and backup candidates are needed. Other times a client may be "fishing" or speculatively running a search that never ends in a hire. The agent ends up just as frustrated as the hopeful job seeker in this case, and it happens often. Use your own professional discretion on which job listings to pursue and know there is a chance you could land a great position as a result, so it is well worth the effort.

Technically there are a few helpful tips you need to know about responding to jobs as well. Number one is discussed above, and it is the most basic: Follow directions! There is nothing worse than a great candidate who makes a simple mistake on the instructions, immediately casting doubt on their true abilities. Second, be very clear about your fit for the *exact* job you applied for. The online job applications are reviewed even more haphazardly than blind resume submissions, so make sure the initial information is targeted. If there is space for an introduction email or letter, it had better state in the first one or two sentences why you are the best choice for the exact role advertised. If we have to dig through your information and make assumptions, it may be too late. Also be careful with language that is "all about you," instead of the employer. Don't frame your responses with reasons the job will be great for you. Instead pinpoint the exact ways you are a fit for what the client is seeking. Last, check and re-check everything before hitting "send" or "submit" buttons. Once these electronic forms go through, there are no take-backs. What you send is what they will evaluate you with. Be certain your presentation is the way you want it to look on the other end! Overall, treat the online job application process as part of the interview. Take it seriously and proceed carefully.

> Author's Note: One of the most damaging offenses in our candidate's online activity is applying for multiple positions at completely different levels with the same advertiser. When we see an application from an Estate Manager coming in for a position of Housekeeper and Nanny we wonder how to take either seriously. Don't make this error. If you need to communicate a range of possibilities in your job preferences, make that clear in your direct conversations with agents. Don't just sloppily apply online for anything that gets posted.

The above is a sampling of what may appear to be slight errors or minor issues. However, at the "expert" or management level these mistakes are taken as evidence of incompetence, lack of knowledge, or simply not caring. It is for mainly that reason we are presenting the common mistakes we see as well as some more picky corrections. A general review of the items will offer you one of two things:

A correction of mistakes you have already made, or a confirmation that your diligence has paid off. Hopefully more will experience the latter, but let's say that the information is given, "just in case." Going over these sections is very similar to the advice we give most candidates preparing for interviews, where we suggest going online and searching for "Top 10 interview mistakes." Refreshing yourself with simple lists of things to pay attention to just might be the difference in your interview and job search success. Most of us know the basics, but we just need to be reminded sometimes!

Working With Domestic Employment Agencies

If you have ever looked for a job in the private service field, there is a good chance you have dealt with a domestic employment agency. If not, your next job search should include at least one agency to represent you. In the mid 2000's we would have advised candidates to work with perhaps two or three agencies exclusively, building a very strong relationship and having those few agents present you with the best possible fit once they know you well enough. These days we recommend a two-fold approach: Have a close relationship with a few agents, preferably in your local area, and then have a controlled distribution effort with as many other resources and agencies as you can manage. There are more agencies and fewer jobs in the current marketplace, so carefully casting a wide net beyond your close contacts will ensure the best chance of results. Whether you have had good or not-so good luck with an agency before, the following tips and information will be very valuable as you approach your new job hunt.

Another upfront issue is how to determine the experience, reputation, or competence of an agency service. This is a great item for networking among associates in the industry, reading online posts in related groups, and also looking for some basic business data. Many agencies are just individuals who form their business practice as an LLC or some other entity to properly conduct agency searches. You can always find company information in the state level governments to see if companies are registered properly and currently as they describe themselves. That also reveals how long they have been in business. It is also possible to have a general phone call introduction to see if there is a good basic match with the type of jobs an agent might represent. For example, if we get a call from a Nanny in Chicago, we would not want their full application, but would review their resume and refer them to a partner or local business to help with their search. It isn't a position that our agency would likely encounter and we'll save the candidate lots of time and effort by steering them to a more appropriate resource. Try to get a sense of the company you choose to work with before sending piles of information. It should be handled sensitively and in close communication with you throughout the process, even if the match doesn't happen with a job right away.

Before proceeding with agency relationships you should understand the agency's function and why they are looking almost exclusively for applicants with years of experience. Domestic agencies get paid by clients to find them skilled employees who have been successful in a home and have the references to prove it. Therefore, an agent tries to present candidates who have recent, well-documented experience in their field and impeccable histories. If you are just starting out or are making a "career change" because a domestic job sounds like something you want to try, forget it. You can, however, call on an agency and kindly ask advice for breaking into the field, but don't expect too much attention. If you want to learn how to get started in the private service industry, or transition from a related field, see our recommended resources in the chapter on "Finding a Private Service Position." (The best target call for inquiring about entry to the field is one of the schools who also handle placement. They are very informative throughout their sales process and enjoy inquiries.) The only exception is if you have skills relative to the work you are looking for, such as high-end hotel management, bed & breakfast, restaurant Chef work, etc. Some agencies accept "entry-level" applicants for clients who may not need an applicant with direct private service experience. It is more rare, but apply to the agencies who encourage you to do so.

If you are a skilled, experienced candidate, start your agency approach with a few basics in place. First and foremost, you can't find something if you don't know what you are looking for. Before you seek an agency to represent you, know for certain what position and what job description you are asking for. If you don't know already, you probably should not use an agency, and if you do know, but can't communicate it well, nobody will be able to assist you to search on your behalf. A great rule of thumb we offer our applicants is this: In thirty seconds, can you explain your job title and what your job search is to a friend who knows nothing about the private service industry? Will they understand and be able to relay that information clearly to someone else? If not, you need some work. Again, when you are trying to be perceived as an expert at what you do, you should be able to "teach" about your position on demand. Though you can expect a successful agent to have knowledge about the position, you need to be the one who consistently communicates exactly the role you fit and describe the many details of your expertise.

Next, when you do contact agencies, be prepared in every way! Don't even call if you don't have a resume. The previous section is your guideline to be ready for the paperwork requirements of just about any employment situation, so use it. Once you are ready, call the agencies local to where you want to work and also try the agencies that place nationwide. The best advice is to register with every agency in the world if you have the time and patience, because each agency gets different clients, and more clients = more jobs! This will take a lot of your own effort, but if you have fully prepared and checked out the agents as discussed earlier, you should be up to the challenge. Also, agencies work for you for FREE, so it is fine to use them all, and never pay an agency to register for employment. Knowing this, it is important to be respectful of the time and any guidance you do receive along the way. Remember, agencies get paid by the employer when you get hired, so trust me, if they have a job that fits your background, you'll quickly become "best friends" through the hiring process.

Author's Note: Don't make the major mistake of playing favorites with agencies. There is a reason our company was named Domestic Placement Network. It's because the way we initially built the agency was in cooperation with like-minded placement agencies across the country. Similar to real estate transactions, a group of us have worked together through the years to successfully extend the reach for our clients and source the best possible candidates. That means we are constantly sharing notes and experiences both good and bad about the candidates we represent. If you have a problem or conflict with one agency, it may affect your status with another. The point is, you'll never know for sure if a random set of agencies work as partners. Make sure you maintain professionalism even in the face of a bad agency experience. Never "badmouth" an agency when you are speaking with another. If it comes up in conversation, you may suggest that you had a less than positive experience at company A or B, but never say anything overly critical. (Even if it is true!) If you have a legitimate, formal complaint about an agency business practice, use the appropriate government and business channels to resolve the issue.

The registration steps for each agency will be different. Some will ask you to fax or email a resume first, then if you are qualified you will fill out the full application. Others will have you do a complete application right away to be considered for representation. Some may not even take your application. Either way, follow the instructions of the person you are in contact with. After submitting the application or resume, allow the agent to get back to you on their time. They may be busy working with placements or more likely do not have a suitable position to talk to you about at the moment. A good rule is to wait 3-5 business days to follow up after you have spoken to or sent something to an agency. Be persistent, but try not to be annoying. If there is a job on an agent's desk that you are perfect for, they will call you immediately and treat you like a long lost friend! Be patient.

Did I mention patience? Let's look at the numbers for a moment: A typical agency has several hundred to several thousand applicant files. Some are computerized, but many are in filing cabinets and are searched manually when a job order needs to be filled. For example, here's what happens when a client calls the agency for a Private Chef:

The client will have specific details about the type of person, cuisine, schedule, living arrangements, salary, etc., that they are looking for. Based on the job details, an agent goes through the files of all available chef candidates for a possible match either by computer search, flipping through applications, or by memory. Out of maybe 100 available applicants, an agent selects just a few to send to a client, maybe four or five. The client reviews the files sent by email or fax and decides whom to interview. And then if a perfect match is found through the interviews only one person gets hired! So if a very busy agency does just two chef placements per month, your chances are about 2 out of 100 or *1 in 50* that you will land a chef position through the agency at any given time. It's not pretty. Many candidates on file with agencies may only get one or two interviews over a span of years, and many more never get interviewed at all.

Here's the trick: Try to be in the four or five applicants sent on every job order at every agency. How? Have the best, most complete, most up-to-date application on file and follow up periodically to have a great relationship with the agents representing you. Basically, it all comes back to the preparation and presentation from the "Better Candidate" section. This is assuming, of course, that you are equally qualified with the other applicants. Likewise, the specific requests of an employer might disqualify you right away, but there is nothing you can do about that. Your only mission is to beat out the other candidates on jobs you are a match for. So be the best applicant in the files and have a solid, ongoing relationship with the person representing you. Always be on the lookout for ways you can set yourself apart from the pack and enhance your profile as a top candidate.

Discrimination?!? Yes.

There, we've said it. Discrimination in the hiring process is rampant. On a number of levels, clients and personnel in the hiring process will have preferences for staff that include or exclude candidates because of age, race, sex, body type, and more. Similar to Hollywood, the hiring of private staff can be more like a movie casting in some homes. The "look and feel" of employees in the home can be a major factor for the employer, considering the staff as an extension of their own image. Some of these decisions are superficial, but some have legitimate qualification. For instance, the age factor can impact the service relationship in a number of ways. Some younger employers have communicated that they would not "feel right" directing the manual labor of an older employee, or being served by someone far more senior out of respect. The long term prospects for a more mature candidate are also considered if the intention is a long term position with the family, and similar considerations apply if there are very demanding physical aspects of the job.

As another example, there may be a particularly conservative, politically connected family who chooses to have staff with similar traits.

In this instance an applicant with a non-traditional relationship may be disqualified. Another important arena for gender preference involves the close personal contact and environment of the employment. Will a male employee be looking after young female children or spending time in the personal bedroom of the Lady of the House? This likely will be served better by a female candidate. Not to mention the numerous possibilities of employers who need a travel assistant, spend time in close quarters with the opposite sex, or other potentially uncomfortable or inappropriate scenarios. Other considerations we deal with from clients are: languages, accents, religious views, past employer associations, makeup and fashion styles, smoking, and more! We are by no means suggesting what is right or wrong on any level here, but we are offering the reality based on thousands of examples over the years.

How we deal with client preferences as an agency will vary. The legal and ethical aspects are for us to manage with appropriate legal counsel, and there are plenty of very good and bad examples of how this is treated among employment agencies. Unfortunately the rules of the game are varied and contain many more gray areas than black and white answers. We have found more often than not that clients who make such requests have little concern for the legal aspects and responsibilities of the agency. Of course this is not a blanket statement, but in general at this level of personal choice and service, the details and specific requests of employers seem to override many of the rules.

As a last note, you should remember that even though agencies can help you, you do not have to take any abuse. You are a human being and professional and should be treated that way. If someone is rude to you without cause, simply don't ever speak to them again. They probably don't have any positions for you anyway if they treat you poorly. No big deal, there are plenty of agencies out there. In turn, have patience when going through the interview process because clients are sometimes flaky and agencies have no control over the schedule. Hang in there and pursue all the opportunities you can. Your only goal is to find the right position for you.

Job Seeker's View: Alan Bussey

We invited Alan to give us a realistic look at the downside of job searching. We have placed Alan in the past with a top Forbes List client of ours, and recently his position was unfortunately consolidated by the family office operations. Since then he has endured a very frustrating and lengthy search for new employment. Alan notes:

"My experience since my latest job in domestic service has been a series of close calls, and just as much frustration in the process. I have been told that to find the right match an agency is involved in a 'Needle in the haystack' type of search. The more interaction I've had, with short, blunt, and straightforward conversation, the more I'm convinced that this is exactly what our headhunting friends are faced with. Comments such as: 'They are really looking for a female,' might stem from a comfort level with the closeness which comes with this level of intimacy, or it might be the result of small girls within the family and a desire to create 'little girl freedoms.' For example, that precious daughter might enjoy waking up, taking all her clothes off, and interacting for her first hour(s) in the buff. Everyone would be more comfortable with a female at this moment... The last scenario would or could be that principal would prefer to interact with a female, just because. I think they have that right, but it doesn't help me find a job! It might be that the most important criteria could be to have 'Midwestern values.' What in the world could this mean, and how would one bring this to the table, or present these skills in a resume? Then there is 'Locals only will be considered.' Is this written to eliminate me, or does someone really think that a local would do this job better than a professional from a different state? There are so many intangibles; and unfortunately, it is about the intangibles... bringing it back to a 'Needle in the haystack!'"

Expert's View: Feigon Hamilton

The following section is from our staffing agency partners Susan Feigon and Gail Hamilton, presented in a conversation format. For more than ten years we have worked together on placements across the country, constantly challenging and assisting each other in our pursuit of the highest standards when dealing with both clients and job applicants. You'll see many areas that overlap or are similar to our book's content, and some points where we may differ. Overall, we thought it was important to offer other professionals' views on such an important section. Enjoy!

Hazing Process: Pulling all your information – the what and why.

So you are looking for a job; you research all options and compile a list of viable contacts, word of mouth, old employers and colleagues, friends/family and agencies. Now you take the time to write your resume, a beautiful cover letter, and send it to everyone. They are happy to review, but when it hits the staffing firms you realize that you have to play the "agency game." "What is this?" you might ask...

Here at Feigon Hamilton we believe that in order for our clientele to feel comfortable interviewing you, we need to know as much about you as possible in order to represent you. "Wow, not just my resume?" you might ask.

> Gail: "You would be in their house, with their children, with their assets, on their property; they are vulnerable so why shouldn't they know who you are and a bit of history longer than the last five years as recommended by most corporate recruiters?"
> Susan: "Gail you are correct, not everyone has security staff on property so it is our job to help protect and secure our clients as best we can."

Submitting a resume is just the beginning; signed and on letterhead, letters of recommendation that can be verified, list of references and contact information, appropriate photograph for your presentation (so many of our clients are interviewing across the nation; it is advantageous for them to have a visual of you), reasons for leaving your past positions and all legal documents supporting the forms that we need for background checks.

> Gail: "Don't forget the application!"
> Susan: "Oh yes, and how about the work samples pertaining to each specific job such as menus for chefs, budget and spreadsheets for estate managers, inventory lists or household manuals for household managers and even carefully crafted letters representing an employer's foundation written by a personal assistant?"
> Gail: "The samples would be just that; samples of work performed in the past but ALWAYS with numbers and names taken out to protect the confidentiality of the past employer."
> Susan: "Right, we are looking for formatting and details on how you capture things and put them together.

It helps us assess an A++ candidate from a B or C and also allows us to share other systems with you so you can enhance your repertoire."

Gail: "We can also glean if you have the skill sets and talents and are ready to move up the ladder in private service. If this is the case, we will mentor you in the process and help market you accordingly for growth."

What else do agencies require? Read on, this is just the beginning of the hazing process! Let's proceed to the next step in being considered for representation in the "agency game."

Hush Hush, Don't Tell: The written word and beyond.

Confidentiality is essential in private service – before, during and after hire. It is imperative to maintain confidentiality throughout the entire process! Let's start with the resume.

Susan: "Right, how many resumes have we seen with dollar amounts in it? You know those types, the ones where people are sharing private information about the cost of a renovation."

Gail: "What about the candidates that share the details of the art collections and automobile collections? Whoa, not something that resonates well with the client. No one should know what is behind closed doors!"

Susan: "Yup, time to write 'auto collection' and not 'Mercedes, Bentley, etc.'"

Gail: "People are always asking us how they are supposed to let a potential employer know that they 'know' how to care for those collections. All I say is that if they have worked for another high net worth employer, it won't matter."

Gail: "Oh and don't forget the clients that negate candidates on the spot due to breach in confidentiality on the resume. Sadly, we have seen our clients cancel face-to-face interviews over this."

Susan: "Frustrating isn't it? Or maybe your mistake is that you *write* things correctly, but in an interview you *share confidentialities*– oops – not good."

Gail: "So, how do you talk about your past employer? YOU DON'T. You talk about your work and your past accomplishments only."

We at Feigon Hamilton always write, "Reason for leaving: _____" on your resume under each position. The client is going to ask it anyway so we like to be proactive. It is nice to have it written where they can see it and reference it. This is another area where keeping confidentiality is crucial.

Susan: "What about someone that has divorced? How do you share that? We don't at all. That is private and privileged information. The best thing you can write is that you were let go due to a change in family dynamics."

Gail: "Sometimes it is broadcast in the newspaper and magazines since they are a public figure; that doesn't mean that you should perpetuate it."

Susan: "Sometimes your past employer gives you permission, says that it is okay to share but we still feel that you would be best served if you kept things confidential."

Gail: "What if they were let go due to financial difficulties?"

Susan: "Are you kidding? That is the same thing as sharing a divorce, it is very private. Please don't share.

Best to say that the family changed its staffing needs. Be polite, be proper and for heaven's sake, show some respect!"

Gail: "What about if they couldn't get along with the principal? Or if they had some very strange lifestyle habits?"

Susan: "Hush, hush, don't tell!!!"

Privacy issues in today's world can also depend on whom you interview with, and your past employers' particular situations.

Gail: "Sometimes you haven't been given permission to disclose your past employer's names."

Susan: "And sometimes you aren't even allowed to know the name of the potential employer you are interviewing with."

Gail: "What about when you are working with multiple agencies and you don't even know that you have applied to the same job over and over again?"

Susan: "We aren't thrilled with that are we Gail? Nothing worse than spending hours and hours working with a candidate, developing their resume, briefing them on the job and finding out after presentation to the hiring representative that they have already been presented by another agency. (Oops, that is another issue but please keep a list of the jobs you have spoken to agencies about so this doesn't happen. They do sound a lot like each other at times but with careful scrutiny, you will notice that it *IS* the same position.)"

Gail: "Agencies want to know who you worked for, yes that means names; full disclosure. We can keep it confidential on your resume by using "Confidential Family" or using the Family Office LLC name but we still need to know because we are representing you to our 'confidential client.'"

Susan: "Another important factor is keeping confidentiality during the interview process. While interviewing it is best to not share the name of the potential employer with anyone (family/friends/agencies) and after you are employed it is best that you use the name of their Family Office LLC they might have created but please try to not say, 'I work for Mr. and Mrs. High Net Worth.'"

Gail: "Hush, hush, don't tell!!!"

Wu Wei – As the Water Flows: Helping Us Help You

Responding to requests from an agency – going with the flow, is crucial. In this instance, "flow" means responding to any and all requests in a timely manner. To create a good agency relationship, keep it professional but warm, accommodating and responsive.

> Gail: "Don't get too close or chummy; this needs to be a professional relationship. Not that we don't like warm and fuzzy, everyone does, but there is a time to keep your boundaries up so we can envision how polished you will be throughout the interview process and eventually, on the job."
>
> Susan: "Also, don't be rude and arrogant – we are working with you and you want us on your side! If not, we have enough other candidates that are respectful. Bottom line; we don't like cocky we like intelligent yet humble!"
>
> Gail: "If you treat us poorly, undoubtedly you will be the kind of gate keeper that will treat the employer's vendors poorly. Not good!"

Susan: "Right Gail, you are representing the employer to the outside world. Only he or she has the right to be arrogant and that is for them to do, not you! The plumber, electrician, gardener, and even the agencies are all vendors and you must be kind and professional. How you treat us is indicative of how you will treat all the vendors for the principal. Not good! Your job is to make sure everyone likes you so they are willing to drop everything to help you out when you call with a last minute request from your principal."

Gail: "Sometimes we get candidates that have an attitude like, 'You need us in order to staff your clients!!' That is true but that attitude won't fly. We do need you but there are 1,000's of others out there. Why have an attitude anyway?"

Ensure ease of communication during a job search; always respond via phone/cell/email in a timely and professional manner, with clarity, even though your day is full with important details and deadlines.

Gail: "Salutation and close on each email. Oh, what a pain you say; we use this as an indicator to show us that you know how to write, and eventually represent your future employer. Bottom line; treat agencies like you would treat your employer or they are unlikely to promote you."

Susan: "Simple email protocol is nice. If we email you, we want a response. Follow through is important even if the answer is short and sweet. There is a lot of sensitive information being transferred back and forth; nice if it is acknowledged."

Gail: "In a timely manner too!"

Susan: "If we send you an email with a job description, be kind enough to respond. Lack of response to us tends to mean that you are not interested, but it is also disrespectful. We might not be inclined to continue to communicate with you in the future."

Gail: "Don't forget about us or ignore us when we write because you will need us eventually. When you are ready to look for a new job, we might not be responsive. We will remember your lack of communication."

Susan: "Also your email address – wow – shaking my head over here – how about the one that was lovedrop@aol.com or prince1934@aol.com? Change your email address to be professional; always keep in mind who is receiving it."

Gail: "Don't forget to keep your professional email address too. Maybe create a domain that you have for the rest of your life. Easier than using one that your internet provider offers. When you move, it can remain the same!"

Susan: "If you keep the same one, all your business colleagues can find you years from now! Once you are in our database, we will always know how to reach you. Hey, don't forget to keep the cell and keep the email consistent."

Gail: "Now that we brought up email addresses that aren't professional, how about outgoing voicemail messages? 'Hi, this is Susie-cakes and Little Johnny and Rover (bark bark), please leave us a message and when we get back from our walk...' PLEASE!!!!"

Susan: "On the phone subject; landlines are not archaic. Don't give up that solid, clear phone that plugs into the wall. Cells/mobiles/whatever you want to call them are sporadic and not reliable. Important calls need to be heard – every word! Example; when we are on the phone with you speaking about a job offer, do you want us to miss half of the information?"

Gail: "Ha, so you asked for $150,000 a year and we only hear $50,000?"

Susan: "Don't drive and talk on your cell, and don't talk when others are around, you can't be too careful. Barking dogs, cats whining, children crying, roommates talking to you at the same time or worst – overhearing what you are sharing when it is supposed to be confidential."

Gail: "If you don't have a landline and the cell reception in your home is horrible, find a spot and stay there. Don't move a muscle – either that or get a landline again!"

Susan: "Continuing on with communication, when we ask a question; please be succinct, get to the point."

Gail: "Long stories make us glaze over at times; can you imagine what the client is going to feel like?"

Susan: "Remember the 3 second rule in the corporate world? Get your point across before the recipient yawns (loses interest). No matter what you think, they won't or don't hear what you are trying to communicate as you drone on."

How should you handle the need for full disclosure on our requests for "classified" information?

Gail: "We will always need very private information from you. We will honor anything you share and keep things confidential! We do need you to disclose the names of your past employers, letters of recommendations will have the employer's name or business name on it too and things need to match. Sharing reasons for leaving with us, even if it is negative is imperative. It is best to be forthright and disclose any red flags in your background!!"

Susan: "We need to know as much as possible so we can represent you correctly. If you don't share and it comes up as a surprise/negative in an interview, we all lose."

Gail: "Remember when we worked on that job where the employer had zero tolerance for traffic infractions as well as credit dings? How many candidates had the job offered to them pending a background check only to find out at the end of the process that their report was not clear?"

Susan: "We always ask. For some reason, people seem to forget that they had a 'seatbelt infraction' or didn't pay a bill and their credit dropped?"

Gail: "Many times if you divulge these issues during the interview process, we can speak to the potential employer first and many times, they will not mind. If it comes up as a 'bolt from the blue' – you have wasted everyone's time – and the employer is not forgiving."

Susan: "Communication and flexibility is also making time to interview, to be coached and to be briefed before an interview. Use us, that is what we are here for and we offer our time graciously."

Gail: "But please take the time to respect us during the interview process. Call/write us after the interview to let them know the outcome. We wait for you – since we have to call the client and need your input first. The client will always ask us what you thought/felt/etc.; don't throw us under the bus!"

One big job search mistake is using *only* agencies and expecting them to take care of your life – putting your job search in their hands...

> Gail: "We are partners in your job search; we do not take over your search."
> Susan: "We are one tool in your tool bag; use us wisely."
> If we don't call you, we don't have anything for you at this time.
> Gail: "Don't make us feel like we aren't your best friends just because you aren't on our speed dial. Bottom line; this is a business and the client hires us to find that perfect A+ employee."
> Susan: "Right-o, you see a job on our job board, you call us, and we tell you that you are not a match – ouch!"
> Gail: "You don't know what is going on behind the scenes. Sometimes we can't put in print that the client is asking for a male only or female only. Trust us! You might not even want the job and we are protecting you."
> Susan: "Some assume if you aren't hearing from us, we don't like you. Not true. It is because we don't have a job that matches right now. Call or write us anyway and stay on the top of our brains for the next amazing job that comes in. Trust us. Really trust us! If we toss a job at you without a lot of details, we love it when our candidates "trust" us and just say, 'Go for it.' If we have been working with you for a while, we will know it is your type of gig."

Last note; when we ask you to revise your resume for a particular job, please do so and quickly. Send it back to us ready for presentation;

correct all typos and grammar yourself. Read it out loud if necessary to make sure it is perfect. *Help us, help you!*

The Intolerables: Reasons we'll be calling you to the carpet!

You don't ever want to receive this type of call, but if you do, we hope that you learn from it! Here are some of the pitfalls and "oops" that have occurred with candidates:

Lying: Plain and simple – DON'T! We will catch you on it one way or the other. You might not think that you are lying but with background checks, references, and a good combing through of your resume (along with your past resumes) we will find discrepancies.

> Gail: "Pretending that you worked at a high end home, you have letters to prove it, phone numbers to call and when we do, we find that the person is a friend of yours that you have coached into lying for you."
> Susan: "How about forgetting to put a past employer on your resume; we are too connected across the U.S., when we dig deep, we find these things out – why leave it out?"
> Gail: "Or we will call a colleague and discover that you were never in charge of hiring or payroll or other management duties - she/he was – do not embellish the truth."
> Susan: "We run background checks; when you said that your driving record was clear and we find that you had a DUI two years ago – what's up with that?"
> Gail: "And how about unpaid taxes, bankruptcies, missed bills all leading to poor credit – and you don't remember this – yes there was a recession but you

need to reveal all situations so we can represent you honestly?"

Susan: "Sometimes we find out that you told your employer one story and us another; we will find out the truth from the employer, from email streams (computers don't lie) and other sources."

Stealing: Sigh,.......really? When found out, you will be banned for life regardless if the family presses charges.

Gail: "We hear employers complain all the time about food being taken that is there for the employer, his/her family or guests, sometimes it is even marked for donations; if it is not yours, has not been given to you, don't touch."

Susan: "Sometimes employers give you a stack of clothing to give to the local charity; not you, the charity – do not think that you can take a piece or two out."

Gail: "Petty cash – do we need to say more – it is not yours."

Susan: "Shopping with family credit card; don't think you can hide your own purchases in the myriad of things you bought and don't lie for heaven's sake and say that you were going to pay for it – don't do it – the accounts get audited all the time."

Gail: "Inventory lists are not to figure out how much the family owns, it is to protect the family from theft; you will be found out."

Susan: "So you think that the employer doesn't know about the rolled up carpets in the storage area of the home? Think again – don't take anything – they are on to you."

Gail: "Food/flowers/liquor after a party; most of the time it is donated, if not, let the family gift it to you or other employees – never ask for it - don't be a schnor (beggar)."

Susan: "Jewelry; hiding your theft and accusing another employee – come on people – we do have eyes in the back of our heads."

Gail: "It is also considered stealing when you work a deal with a vendor to up-charge your employer only to get him/her to do something for you for free or pay you in kick-backs."

Pet Peeves and More Intolerables

Gail: "When we call to check in with you on the job, don't be defensive, we are here to help – share what is going on, the problems and challenges – we can help guide you."

Susan: "Don't go to an interview after drinking gallons of coffee and then asking the potential employer to use the facilities BEFORE you sit down to talk - hold it or don't drink."

Gail: "If you are being interviewed by your potential employer and they offer you a drink, take it politely, thank them but remember your etiquette - don't guzzle, look for a coaster and never let drinking get in the way of your interview – if you can't juggle drinking and talking - oh never mind, just take a sip and leave it there."

Susan: "Controlling the interview; we do believe in the candidate asking a lot of broad questions to get the vision of what the employer wants, but don't avoid their questions or answer a question with a question – dancing around makes you look like you are lying or hiding something."

Gail: "It is all about them, it is never about you. You need to be on your employer's agenda."

Susan: "Boundaries!! Remember there is a paycheck between you, you are not their friend no matter how warm and fuzzy it feels - too close could get you fired – keep a professional but warm presence at all times."

Gail: "Subject line in your email - write something in that box that pertains to the contents of your email if you want us to open and read it."

Susan: "Don't interrupt the interviewer or us when we are talking; stop, listen, absorb and then ask questions or comment."

Gail: "Take notes; we are giving out valuable information."

Susan: "Answering job ads and job board listings; remember which ones you have responded to! If you seem confused you don't look professional and we will make note of this – the little details are what makes the private service professional an A++ player. Not keeping track shows that you are not meticulous and in fact, not respectful of our time."

Cheerleaders: Your advocates before, during, and after employment.

Remember, we are on the sidelines, we are the wind in your sails, and we are your best supporters and promoters.

Gail: "We want you to be successful."

Susan: "We are here to help you through the interview process as well as through the integration process when you start a new job."

Gail: "We understand the clients, your principal, and what they are looking for."

Susan: "Sometimes you get too close to see the big picture, so we are here to help you navigate."

Gail and Susan: ***"This is not a dress rehearsal, it is your livelihood, your foundation, and we don't want you to lose anything that you want!"***

Private Service Employers
Privacy? Please...

Over the years one theme has remained constant in any employer's request for help: They want to maintain their privacy. In fact, many homes and estates are built with that as a main purpose. Sprawling households and grounds are often transformed into luxury retreats with the full accouterments of the finest resorts and hotels in hopes that having your own facilities will keep you free of public interaction. Though having your own golf course, massage rooms, expansive bedroom suite, private art gallery, or hidden poker room may seem to offer the 'hideaway" feeling, it can actually be quite the opposite! The more space and private facilities an employer constructs, the more they will find themselves overrun with staff and vendors at every turn. The simple maintenance and operation of a large estate requires full disclosure to at least a few trusted individuals, if not to an array of construction, repair, and service personnel. The more complex the lifestyle becomes, the more people will need to know what you are up to in your private life. This tends to be one of the great disappointments of wealth at the highest levels. As your home and social lives continue to expand, the number of people making your arrangements and coordinating the upkeep grow accordingly. We even hear the occasional rant about grand properties becoming virtual prisons for employers who want nothing more than to be left alone. I recall a tale of one employer who chose to have full A/V and telephones installed in their closet, where they ended up spending most of the day to be away from the household staff!

We say all of this to be honest with ourselves in the process of employing staff. There is no such thing as complete privacy, so hiring private staff needs to be treated with the utmost care. The people working for you in your personal lives will be privy to all of your secure data, relationships, habits, good and bad days, and many of your lifelong secrets. With this understanding, you can choose whom to trust in the process, rather than not trusting anyone. We are honored to be in a position to hold your lifestyle information confidentially as agents for your private hiring, and don't take it lightly. We have non-disclosure agreements in place with many of our clients, and operate with that level of discretion whether there is a written contract or not. We assist clients in maintaining privacy throughout the staffing process, only revealing pertinent information as appropriate, and with permission. Of course there will be some mistakes over the years, but believe it or not, they usually come from the clients themselves! As an additional consideration, without fail, the more high profile a client is in the mainstream media, the more problems they will have with hiring and maintaining private staff. The many aspects of privacy and service flow become daunting when things like personal security and paparazzi enter the mix. The estate owner will ultimately have to give up some control to their staff and communicate their desired results along the way.

Expert's View: Glenn Greenhouse, Greenhouse Agency, Ltd.

Glenn is a long time, New York based staffing professional who has seen many waves, trends, and changes over the years. He recently wrote about some of the difficulties new clients are facing.

"If only Employers of 'Personal Service Staff' would be clear about their expectations and the job.....what a wonderful world it would be????

I've found the majority of my clients have found (learned) ways of making tons of money.... but along with this comes the "Frankenstein"...... the 15,000 + sq. ft. house or apartment. The 2nd and 3rd (many times more) properties. Boats, planes and a fleet of cars. But these are still family units, with the same basic needs of all families, compounded now with complications of all the toys mentioned above. It's a "monster" resulting from hard work, success & choice of lifestyle.

Now eight or more bathrooms need cleaning, four or more beds need be stripped and made if not the linens changed entirely, thousands of sq. ft. of floors needed vacuuming -moping-sweeping-waxing-washing, god only knows how much glass/mirrors to be Windexed.....all each and every day. This is just scratching the surface of the multitude of tasks and work requiring attention and responsibility..... each and every day!

Proper and professional management is now a necessity. The Principal/s must detail their 'wants and wishes,' being clear about their expectations.

So many of my clients have told me; 'I wish we were back in our smaller Park Ave apartment. I never had to deal with all this staff,' or 'We have so much money, but we really are not happy because we can't find the right staff to do the needed jobs, tasks and take on the necessary responsibilities, so that we can truly enjoy what we have.'

Well....we suggest you give up a bit of control and hire the right House-manager, PA etc..... A professional!

It's literally; 'watch out what you wish for, you just might get it.' A 'Frankenstein situation' was created and it's hard to control. It's funny how some people can manage 'conglomerates,' but not their homes. I feel for lots of my clients, because it is a tough job. They have 2 – 4 kids of different ages. Being rich, these kids are involved in a multitude of activities and their social lives require a PA to manage. Laundry in these houses is a full-time job in itself. What about meals, while Mom & Dad are on crazy diets or eating one type of cuisine, while the kids are finicky and must be served something else altogether. I can go on and on.

Communicating with Staff is absolutely essential. Outlining chores and schedules is a must. Securing proper quality and experienced staff goes without saying. So......if the boss takes the time to be clear with how their house should be run, along with their expectations....VIA their designated manager, then he/she will see to it; a smooth running operation is in place. Hopefully the end result is a "wonderful world" with satisfied Principal/s and a happy staff."

Client Self-Sabotage

When it comes to privacy, searching for, and hiring private staff, many clients commit mistakes they may not even be aware of. Having the unique perspective of running both an agency and the top job board site for private staff, we get to see an overall view of clients' staffing efforts. A number of private employers use online advertising and recruiters to find staff for their homes. These job listings online are very effective but also present some challenges. One of the worst cases is seen when recruiting to replace current staff. How can you keep the advertisement general enough so they don't identify their own jobs on the site? That's a tough one. Another challenge is being able to effectively communicate the needs of the home or the details of the position. Without experience in advertising for private staff, the actual ad may be incomplete or misleading (unintentionally). Also, if you don't work closely with the staff member's position, you may not know all the duties and elements to require of new applicants. In the same way, using the wrong type of recruiter or agent may produce insufficient results. The vocabulary and necessary elements of the process need to be drawn out by a seasoned employer or agent with years of know-how in this specific field. Likewise, when communicating the needs of the employer to potential staff, the right representative who is "speaking the same language" is key.

For these and many other reasons we recommend using a qualified domestic agency or household professional to assist with any private service staffing. One would never bring the Ferrari down to the Hyundai dealer for an engine rebuild, so why wouldn't you ask for the advice of an expert on something as critical as staffing your home? Sure, there are some exceptions, but in general, we don't expect the principals of the estate to know everything about running the place. And you shouldn't have to! So start from an expert view. Depending on the level of services required, it is always best to work from the top down, hiring an Estate Manager or House Manager to configure the appropriate staffing based on your preferences. From this platform the hiring map can be laid out and the search can be conducted with specific positions conceptualized. As an alternative, in certain situations an owner can call upon a "consultant" or estate management professional to assess their needs and guide the hiring framework. In recent years through the proliferation of internet and social media, many top estate personnel have been able to offer their services "a-la-carte" and help clients create staff descriptions, household manuals, train employees, or find new staff. Either way, we highly recommend having a knowledgeable expert on your side as you build a private service team.

Similar issues arise when trying to convert a business hiring approach to the household environment. We regularly work with clients' employees in their businesses who are tasked with finding private staff. Whether an HR director, Accountant, Attorney, or company VP, chances are that they won't have the knowledge to fulfill your needs correctly and efficiently. There are so many different criteria, nuances, and procedures for employing private staff that a client's business hierarchy usually messes up the flow. Those representing employers in this instance may actually misinterpret the requests and criteria for the private hires due to a lack of understanding of the terminology or the estate environment. The efforts of everyone can be wasted if several layers of screening happen without expert knowledge, only to find that the employer has no interest in a candidate who has been through several rounds of preliminary interviews. Again here we recommend a consulting approach whether hiring an independent professional to assist or working with a top agency. The general rule of thumb is, like in the Ferrari example, you probably want someone who has "been there and done that" in the private service realm.

Author's note: Just as we spend much of our time at the agency screening candidates, there is a discernment necessary in taking on clients as well. There happens to be a number of client names that are "known" in our business as extremely difficult or "revolving doors." You don't want to be on this list. There is a very small network of professional domestic agencies that often work together in friendly collaboration for the benefit of clients, and we can receive negative information about clients when our candidates interview through our partners. There are also very few places that jobs are advertised for private service, so if the same "known" client's jobs keep appearing month after month, year after year, then we know something is not right. Likewise, even though most employees are very confidential and kind in what they share about past employers, seeing the same client name on dozens of resumes for the same positions makes it easy to see a difficult employment history. We have many employees who know about difficult clients because of their interviewing habits as well. Especially in smaller towns and cities, if an employer is constantly meeting applicants for the same positions, the local talent pool will be turned off. We regularly hear statements like, "If the job is with Mr. and Mrs. (Insert bad employer name here), then forget it!" If you feel like you may have dealt with several agencies and staff on the same positions, there may be opportunity to hire a consultant and see if some adjustments can be made to your staffing process.

Your Own Worst Enemy — Do You Even Care?

Expert advice can only go so far. Over time we've seen some fantastic employers who follow the "letter of the law" when hiring and compensating staff. Others, however, have done everything from paying substandard wages to egregiously violating labor law, and even involving staff in blatant criminal activity. Let's assume you are not on the extreme side of breaking the law, but perhaps in a place of necessary evaluation of your employment practices. In this case, we encourage you to be educated about the rules (both federal and state) to do things right. Our company is not in a position to give legal advice, but we can certainly recount story after story of employers ending up in court or having to settle for large sums of money due to violations. This only applies, of course, if you care! Many employers know what they want, and exactly how they want to go about it. Your situation will be unique.

I can't be sure, but it appears that some UHNW clients skirt the law for "sport," because sticking to the guidelines would often take little or no more effort and money. So here's the warning: Private Service workers are becoming very knowledgeable about labor laws, discrimination, and all the requisite legal ramifications. There is simply no need to test the water on this issue. Even if you can ultimately prevail in any legal challenge because of superior resources, there is no good reason to take the shortcuts. You'll end up with publicity you don't want and more headaches than necessary. A few major points to watch: *Don't pay in cash. Don't hire undocumented workers. Be reasonable with hours and overtime. Hire extra staff if necessary*. Do the right thing, and hire an expert with specific knowledge in household employment for your state. We are happy to refer you to the best.

Expert's View: Julie Kroubetz

Julie Kroubetz is an Estate Management Consultant and staffing partner of our firm. She has a number of years of experience in private service and has worked on several staffing assignments with our agency. We asked Julie to add her views on the issues facing clients as they decide on and communicate what they want out of private service staff.

"I want 5 star hotel style service in my home" is a recurring request from clients. Really? Are you sure? Okay then, how do you go about obtaining that high level of service? The critical factor is to know how to ask for what you want and then accept the terms that may go along with achieving that goal. The saying of being careful of what you wish for should make you pause enough to give this wish some deep thought. Like most things in life, it's hard to have a thought, snap your fingers and have it happen almost by magic. If you want to upgrade your style of living to any level, including 5 star, there is a way to plan for it so that you get exactly what you want.

Here are the things to consider: First you must identify what 5 star means to you personally. This is by far the most important step of your upgrade plan. Think about what services you have enjoyed and how they made you feel. Is that service something that you would appreciate each and every day, or is it something that is special and should only be realized when you travel or rest in a luxurious external environment? Write down the things that you would want and then think about it some more to determine if your lifestyle meshes with the service. For example, if you love the formality that some 5 star service offers but your household is a barefoot, casual home riddled with children, pets and homey chaos, then this style of service may not be suitable for this time in your life. Years ago, a very prominent potential client was interested in having me come in to establish organization and serenity. Prior to meeting with the client I was able to do some research by reading a few biographies that had been written about the client. Different authors established the same theme of daily chaos and higher than normal energy within the home. Why would a client in their later years of life want such a drastic change I wondered. After some careful consideration, it became evident that the client believed that they wanted this change, but in all actuality it was only wishful thinking. The client would not be able to change their lifelong pattern to live this new way no matter how appealing it looked. So you really must know who you are, who else impacts your life and household and then you can identify the exact 5 star services that fit into your life without you needing to change yourself or others to fit into a 5 star life. The art of living well is determined by what you establish of what works for you, be it elegant or casual.

Once the services that you want to have in your home have been determined, you need to know how to ask for those services and set service expectations. You must be extremely specific in what you want and expect. If you want a room that you spend your time in to always looks pristine each and every time you enter it, consider how that will work. You will turn over the task of making this happen to your staff, but you need to have a part in laying the plan because you are the affected person. If you are in this room a lot during the day and only leave it for food or restroom breaks but want it freshened and cushions plumped when you return a few minutes to an hour later, then you need to think how that could happen. Do you ring for service or just expect staff to anticipate your needs. If staff is to anticipate your needs, they may need to hover near you at all times and you must be completely comfortable with that since it could infringe on your privacy. If you don't want someone lurking around waiting to tend to your every need, then you would need to signal your need and that could become an irritation over time because you are always having to ask for something.

You can have whatever you want. You just have to know what it is that you truly want, how to successfully ask for and obtain what you want and then be willing to pay the financial price for it. 5 star service does not come cheap. If you go behind the scenes of a luxury hotel offering 5 star service, you will find extremely well trained and cared for staffing that is layered to ensure quality control. You have the worker bee, the worker bee supervisor and the managerial supervisor and then in many cases you have the fourth white gloved, detail driven 'The buck stops with me' supervisor. While traveling with a client, I stayed in the Presidential suite of a 5 star hotel in LA. While my client was out shopping for the day, I stayed in the suite to work for the day. The number of staff coming thru that suite from the moment the cleaning started until the room was cleared for preparedness for my client was impressive. As noted above, there were two housekeepers tending to the rooms. While they were cleaning, their supervisor came in to check on them and to see if there were any extenuating issues that needed attention. After that, another supervisory person came in to double check the cleaning process and to ensure that the room amenities were correct and in place. The final visit was from the white gloved inspector giving the stamp of approval that the suite met their standards. Overkill? No. That's usually what it takes to meet 5 star standards!

Hiring Private Service Staff

Conducting the search for top level domestic staff can be a long, frustrating process. However, with a simple strategy the process can be less tedious and produce excellent results. This chapter focuses on the important factors and steps an employer should follow for the best results when searching without the assistance of a placement agency.

One of the most important considerations in staffing is the overall management flow. When hiring a full range of staff, we've seen over time that hiring "from the top down" is key to initial and long term success. A solid Estate or House Manager should have the skills and hands-on experience to help hire, train, and manage the services to the home, whether in a full time capacity or through part time vendors. One of the pitfalls that we see happen frequently is when a new manager (and new management structure) are put in place with a number of support staff already onboard. Unfortunately there is almost always some "push back" rather than cooperation when entrenched staff have new standards imposed on them. Be very sensitive of this during your search for a management level employee. Spend some time in the interview process getting to know their management style, and ask directly how they will approach the position in relation to the other staff.

Our bottom line advice for finding staff on your own is this: If you have the time and expertise available in your own organization, you can certainly complete the search on your own. However, if the burden of time or learning the ins-and-outs of the hiring process create more difficulties, then hire an expert to assist.

The Hiring Procedure (Do-It-Yourself / No Agency)

Plan

Most successful endeavors begin with a clearly defined plan, and so should the hiring process. Set specific goals for all the factors of the hire including time frames for each step of the process and the desired outcome at each stage. Many business authors would note "If you fail to plan, plan to fail." It can certainly apply here. Also, be very honest with yourself and don't make unrealistic goals that set you up for failure. You may get very lucky with the first applicant on the first day or you may have to go through fifty candidates over several months to find just the right fit. Either way, a plan with realistic time frames can make finding great staff as simple as 1-2-3.

Define

The more details in a job description, the easier it is to find a matching candidate. Spend a great amount of effort making a list of every specific function you will expect of the employee and all associated factors. This is the critical foundation for the rest of the search, and as you will see, can save time in other steps. There are a tremendous number of items involved with a proper job description. Many corporate jobs, even at the most basic level may need a five or more page description of all the relevant tasks and qualifications. A private service position can be even more complex with the variations and importance of personality matching, so take great care in preparing this information. It will also be helpful in creating an Employment Agreement and a household or employee manual later on. As indicated earlier, the simplest indicator of long term success is how well the expectations of both employer and employee are communicated from the start. A sample questionnaire form is available through our agency to help with the definition step. Call us if you would like a fillable PDF version emailed to you free.

Reach Out

Once you know what you are looking for it is time to reach all the potential sources you can. The best way to find employees, without question, is by referral. Look to your friends, family, and peers for recommendations of former or current staff who may be looking for a new position. Let those who you can trust know your specific search criteria so they can rattle their brains and be "on the lookout" for possible sources. Second, try to target specific advertising areas for the type of employee you seek. Using classified ads is a good way to see a large selection of resumes, and even better is an industry specific job site like EstateJobs.com. Wherever you decide to advertise, be specific with requirements that are not negotiable. For example, if you want a trained Chef, state it in the ad. The same goes for any unchangeable part of the job and items you will not waiver on. We also highly recommend stating a legitimate salary range and what it is based on. For example, you don't want replies from a $150k per year Estate Manager for a $60k per year House Manager role. Another important detail is to never list a phone number in an ad, just a fax number or email address for resumes. A professional job site or classified listing should allow a way to post anonymously with all responses being directed to your email via a proxy service automatically. EstateJobs.com and Craigslist.org both do this. This will allow you to control whom to speak with once you know a bit about their qualifications, and will avoid random, inquisitive calls about the position.

Legal Note: Pay attention to advertising laws for employment in your state and particular household organization. The wrong language in an ad can lead to complaints, fines, and at the least, turn off some potentially great employees.

Review

At this point you should already have the job description and a picture in your mind of what the perfect employee will be. Now, after hopefully receiving a "stack" of resumes from your advertising, you can begin matching the candidates' skills and background with your ideals. There are many technical factors you can use to judge the applicants, but your first concern should be the job history of the candidate. Look for any significant positions that sound similar to the one you are trying to fill, and consider those first. The best match for your position will be the candidate that has proven him or herself in a job with the same duties you will be asking them to do. Just this simple matching should produce the top candidates for your job, even though you will consider several other elements of the person's history. Evaluation of candidates' resumes is another topic worthy of its own book, so for our purposes we'll continue with the next step assuming you have identified the strongest applicants.

Respond

Once you have selected two or three potential candidates from the resume screening you can begin the preliminary interviews. The first step is to make contact by telephone and set up a time for an in-depth discussion. (Hint: It is great to catch an applicant a bit off-guard and hit them with a few quick interview questions when you call to arrange the formal time. This will give a candid glimpse into how they handle on-the-spot pressure and attitude. As an agent I often disqualify people on how they answer my calls from different numbers or caller ID's.) Set times with all the candidates you want to speak with in this way and you might be able to eliminate one or two based on their phone manner. Now you have a few appointments and a bit of time to prepare. As a courtesy to the applicants you are sure you will not interview further you can either make a quick phone call to let them know the position is filled, send them a letter, or send an email indicating the same. This may be a bit overwhelming depending on the number of resumes you receive, but it is a very nice surprise for job seekers to hear back from an employer even with a rejection. Keep all the resumes with good notes about the source of the candidate for future reference or a new job opening.

Interview

The appointment time has arrived and the first formal interview is about to begin. Are you ready? Do you know how to get the most meaningful information from a candidate? Will you give enough of the right details for the candidate to confirm their interest? This stage is the most important of the entire process without question and many people get caught up in conversation that is misleading or irrelevant to the success of the match. Make sure you know how to interview properly! The next section of the book discusses guidelines that are very helpful for getting the most out of your interviews with a clear understanding of whether or not you are bringing the right person into your home. Putting in the extra time to interview well will pay off later on. You might also consider some modern tech tools for your interview process. The popularity of web cameras, smart phones, and matching services like Skype and FaceTime can help get an overall impression of candidates through a video interview. Many clients prefer the face-to-face interaction, even if it is initially on a video screen.

Final Interviews

The last step with potential candidates is the in-person interview. Even if there was a phone meeting, there are many reasons to interview again in person, and specific techniques to get the most out of the session. The details of effective personal interviewing are beyond the scope of this guide, but the notes on basic interview procedures will apply nicely. Just remember to take as much time as necessary to feel that you really know the person you are considering. Can you see them as part of your family's daily surroundings? Will you be able to relate to this person comfortably for many years? These are very tough decisions and they deserve your time. Similarly, you need to give the prospect as much of a real picture as you can for them to evaluate the job. There is nothing worse than a new employee who uncovers a multitude of reasons they should not have taken the job, just because they didn't get to see it in the interview process.

Verify

If you follow the interview guidelines in this book you will end up with lengthy notes about each candidate you spoke with and you'll have no doubt about what was said by whom. Compare notes on each interview to make a decision on one or two final candidates. You'll now have two of three tools for making the final hiring decision: The resume and the interview results. The third will come from the verification stage of the process. Verification of the candidate's resume information is the final step in your decision criteria. This includes a few different processes depending on what level of checking you want to attempt. One of the important screening tools is employment reference checking, so the next section contains a detailed procedure for doing it effectively. Finding out what a former employer has to say about the candidate can be the most revealing item in the applicant's profile. The other information worth researching is an educational claim such as college or a specialized training. Based on the results of the verification stage you can decide whom you wish to interview in person.

Decide

Finally, with all critical information in your hand and on your mind, make a decision. It is possible to over think the situation with all the factors to consider, but try to make a firm decision and follow it through. If you have done all you can to find the right person you should feel excited about the new employee coming aboard. In fact, you should feel relieved that the process is near an end. Decide who gets the offer and prepare to contact them either with a written letter or by telephone. Doing both is probably your best course so you can be personable on the phone and all business in the written form. A letter will also eliminate any chance of miscommunication over the phone. Likewise, if any negotiation is to take place, all the items will be laid out in detail in a letter that can be revised as the agreement is made.

Finalize

Congratulations! You have successfully made it through the hiring of your new employee. The offer has been accepted and you have set a start date. The last step, which you should make clear to the employee, is the final background investigation phase. This is where you can run any number of additional checks on a candidate to screen for the following:

-Driving History
-Criminal History
-Past or Current Lawsuits
-Education Credentials
-Social Security Verification
-Credit History (If applicable. Check with your state laws for employment background screening.)

It should be made clear that the hiring of the employee is contingent upon any reports that you choose to run on them. This protects you from hiring someone who seemed great all the way, but may have some hidden problems in the past. For instance, if you are hiring an employee that will drive extensively you want to check for DUI's or accidents on their record. Similarly, if the candidate will handle any finances you might want to know if they have a good credit record of their own. Choose relevant items to the situation and of course check to see if they have any criminal history. The internet can offer a number of background searches to choose from, but your best bet for a thorough job is to work with a service on referral. Some agencies are happy to run this process for you "a-la-carte," charging fair rates to pull a complete report as if they had placed the applicant with you. Our firm offers this service upon request and can offer a variety of detail based on your needs.

Welcome.

You now have all the makings of a solid employment situation. It is time to welcome your new employee into your home comfortably, knowing you have done all the right checking and screening. Further considerations should include the start of a "paper trail" for the lifetime of the employer / employee relationship. Some of these items are:

-Confidentiality Agreement
-Written Employment Agreement
-I-9 Form for Identification and Tax Withholding
-Any relevant Manuals or Service Schedules

Once again, if you do not have these resources at hand or already in place, a competent agency or consultant can produce the items for you. In fact, it is not a bad idea to go over these documents before you begin your search so you'll know what the desired end product is.

Long-term success with staff will rely heavily on the initial foundations of the relationship. The more you do here, the more you can refer to later to judge the results of your decision and the performance of the employee. Nobody can meet your needs if they don't know what your needs are! Likewise, without a clear understanding of your employee's expectations for growth, raises, benefits, and future duties, you will not know how to successfully manage and compensate over the long term. Communication is paramount. Hopefully your hard work will pay off with staff that becomes part of your life, blending into your service style and joyfully caring for you and your family for many years to come.

Finding Staff through an Agency

The alternative to conducting your own search for staff is to use a domestic employment agency. There are many benefits to searching with the help of an agency and many employers would not even consider other options. The only drawback is cost, with agency fees varying based upon the salary of the employee you hire. The rest of the chapter will give you a look at why agencies are valuable, leaving you with a simple equation: do the benefits of the agency equal the value of your time and money spent doing the search yourself?

Step by Step Expertise

From start to finish an experienced placement agent can guide you through the hiring process. Chances are that an agent has placed similar service staff in another home very much like yours. They will know to bring up all of the important details concerning the position, type of personality, and work environment that make a successful placement. So the beginning or planning phase of your hiring process requires only your response to standard questions a counselor knows to ask. As you continue through the steps to find staff the agency will have suggestions pertaining to your situation that should save time and make your part very simple. Likewise, the agent will do all of the legwork, compiling the paperwork, screening the candidates thoroughly, and coordinating telephone and in-person interview schedules. They are also the perfect "buffer" in sensitive discussions between the employer and potential employees. They can be impartial and very candid with questions about personal items and salary negotiations, helping get to the point right away.

Reach

The placement agency has its greatest advantage over the individual when it comes to reaching top candidates. Most agencies market to candidates 24/7 in various publications, by constant referrals, and other direct advertising, resulting in a tremendous pool of applicants in an ever-expanding database. The individual performing a one-time search is limited to the area and time where they are searching, and will not know about the many candidates available elsewhere. This reason alone is the basis for the agency fee. The company's overhead is based on the continual updating and searching for qualified candidates to be on "standby" for the employer with specific requirements. So a client is really not paying for the hours it takes to handle their one placement, but for the cost of keeping an "inventory" of candidates.

Selecting an agency should be based on the type of position you are trying to fill. The higher the level of applicant needed, the more reach you'll want. There are several agencies that are capable of placing staff nationwide and some even worldwide. Check with a few agents to determine if they are comfortable to talk to, understand your needs, and have made similar placements. You might also want to use several companies to have a larger pool of candidates to review. Some agencies charge an upfront fee to begin the search for you, while others only bill once you have made a successful hire. You might also consider an agency that is able to access candidates through partner or split agreements with other agencies. This will save you from having to work with more than one person on your search and will avoid the same resumes coming from more than one source. Most high level positions will require the reach of a national agency, but some of the "support" positions are better served locally. These include live-out or part-time childcare and housecleaning. A local agency will typically have a selection of employees within driving distance that can be replaced quickly if necessary. Check your local yellow pages for their ads.

Screening Experience

The employment agency's second function is screening the applicants they attract. Every day resumes and profiles reach the desk of a recruiter and have to be reviewed for their potential success in a new position. This is where the most time savings are offered to the client. Extensive files are created on each qualified applicant, preliminary interviews are done and strengths and weaknesses assessed to determine where they will be a good match. An agency will present a client with only the applicants they know are a fit for the position requirements and the personality of the household. Doing so allows an employer to skip the entire preliminary review process of the random resumes they would find advertising a position on their own. They need only be concerned with identifying the strongest applicant among the few carefully matched profiles from the agency. Also because the agency is continually interviewing, checking references, and compiling documents, the time from start to finish on a top-level hire is greatly reduced.

Sample Agency Timeline

Day 1

Contact one or more agencies to discuss your staffing needs. You should have a very detailed job description to give the recruiter or they can walk you through the creation of one. Have the agency contracts sent by email or fax to review terms and fees, and return signed agreements to those you wish to work with. (If a fee is due to initiate a search you may be asked for a credit card payment or to submit payment by check.) If there is an upfront registration or retainer, make sure you are clear on what to expect in return. Many clients are hesitant about paying upfront, but if you are working with a reputable agency I can assure you they are doing a tremendous amount of work on your behalf from day one. Interact with them frequently and ask many questions along the way. It will be more than worth any upfront costs, and all fees paid likely apply toward the full placement upon hire.

Day 2

The agency begins its search for qualified candidates that match your criteria. Files could be forwarded to you as early as the afternoon you return a signed agreement. It is more likely, however, that an agent will contact each candidate that seems to fit the position and re-interview them for the specific job. They will also verify the applicant's availability and desire for the position. This step could go on for days or even weeks depending on the level of skills and unique characteristics necessary. An agent should have a good idea of who is immediately available within 24-48 hours. If the initial candidates are not suitable, more resources may be employed, such as contacting other partner agencies for resumes or placing specifically targeted advertising for the job.

Day 4-5

Ideally, within a few business days, you will be presented with a few top choices form the agent's files for you to review. It is not uncommon to end up hiring the first or second applicant you see, because the work of the recruiter can bring the best match right to the top of the list for you. Don't be afraid of the "one and done" scenario. When locating unique people in a specific job niche the goal is to find a suitable match and hire! Comparison shopping for staff is not the best way to produce results, and sometimes causes the loss of a great candidate. Again, consult closely with your staffing professional to make these decisions.

Day 6-7

At this stage, assuming you have received candidates that interest you, it is time to conduct interviews. Most employers speak with potential applicants by phone before meeting them in person. This is a wise idea, especially if you have to fly the prospect from another location to meet with you. By speaking on the phone you will identify the top one or two candidates to meet in person. Make travel and interview arrangements with the help of the agent or directly with the applicant yourself. It is normal and expected that all travel costs will be paid by you, the employer throughout the interview process.

Day 7-14

Conduct extensive in-person interviews with the selected candidates. Go through all of the preparation and steps suggested in the chapter on interviewing and clearly discuss all elements of the job while they are on the property. Misunderstandings about employer expectations are the greatest reason for employees leaving a new job. Make sure everyone is clear on all the details of the position. Also consider a "working interview" where a candidate can visit you for consecutive days and perform work as part of your screening process. This is most common with Chefs who will do trial cooking periods for potential employers. Anytime a person works for you, even for the sake of an interview, you must pay for their services. Arrange this in advance through your agency.

Day 14-21

Make a decision on the best employee for your needs and lifestyle, and make a formal offer. It is best to put it in writing, either right away or as a follow-up to a verbal communication of the deal. There should not be much haggling because the financial terms of the offer will be very close to the amount previously discussed with the agency and the candidate. Once the candidate accepts, set a start date and arrival time if they are traveling or relocating. Then consult with the agency to finish official background reports and identification paperwork on the new employee. All offers should be conditional on the final verification of background and references. Again, your agent can guide you through these steps. They should also be able to provide templates and help you draft all necessary documents for a proper offer and hire.

Day 21-30

Mission accomplished! Help the new employee get settled in their position and possibly the new living quarters. Welcome them to your home and give them the necessary equipment, paperwork, and information for their job. Also have a meeting with other staff to introduce the new person and explain their fit within the team. Work closely with them to convey your preferences and service needs from the start. Developing a "custom" employee will be much easier than trying to correct differences later on.

One exception to this average timetable is the Trial Period. Should you want to hire a candidate that is not presently working or that can be flexible with time off from their current job, a one or two week trial period is a good idea. This is especially relevant in positions that require cooking or specialized knowledge such as formal service. If you choose to have a trial, make sure the terms are clear, including the pay, the functions, and the schedule expected during the week(s). You can make a formal offer to a candidate during or after the trial period.

As a final note, if you don't already have it in place, protect and simplify the employment relationship with a payroll service. The right professional service can implement all the legal paperwork and ongoing payroll processing for you. There are a number of easy options to set up things like automatic deposit, check delivery, taxes and withholding, etc. It's really a no-brainer! Please ask us for a referral based on your location and particular needs.

Interviewing Candidates

Finding the best employees can be tricky, and if you don't have the right interviewing skills, you risk losing a brilliant candidate or hiring a person that's not qualified for the job. In addition, while you're sizing up a candidate, that person is also considering you as a potential employer. It is good to ask the right questions, but understanding how to interpret the answers is even more important. When working with an agency it is best if the people screening candidates have either a background working in a household or many years of experience making successful placements.

The following items can help you effectively screen the candidate, make a good impression, and ensure that the candidate gets the information they need about the job and you as an employer.

Have a purpose.

Hiring the right person is the goal of interviewing, but not necessarily the purpose of an interview. An interview is your chance to collect information about the candidate sitting in front of you. It's your opportunity to find out if the applicant is qualified for a particular job, if they are truly interested in the available position and if they fit your personal service style. For candidates that came through an agency it is more important to assess the personality match than the skill set, because they should already be qualified based on your job description. However, use this face-to-face meeting to question the candidates "on the spot" about specific functions they will be doing for your household. Their reactions may tell how they will

approach certain tasks, and whether they are qualified to do them or not.

What's most important?

Many standard interview questions sidestep what you really need to
know - how the person will perform in a specific role. To find and
hire great employees you have to adopt smart interviewing tactics
that uncover a candidate's abilities, talents, strengths and weaknesses, and most importantly, their personality. You practically have to
live with full-time help, so know in advance how you are going to get
along as people. You should have other staff meet with and interview
candidates as well. Many employees bond with one another and will
reveal information that might not come up otherwise. You'll also
discover if the person is a "talker", revealing things they shouldn't or
immediately gossiping too much.

Write down your questions.

Put together a list of interview questions that will help you learn
more about the candidate. Construct open-ended questions that
invite candidates to share information and talk about their experiences. Try to get a feel for how the applicant will deal with actual
situations that have happened or will happen in your home. Use be-
havior-based questions to discover how a person handled a situation
in the past and to determine how they'll react to a similar situation
in the future. Try posing questions such as "Tell me about a time
that... and how did you manage the problem?"

Be ready for questions.

Make sure you give adequate information when answering a candidate's questions. The right details about what they will be asked to

do and how will let them make an accurate decision if the job is right for them. You never want to have an employee say, "I was not aware that was part of my job." Be clear from the start and you will know you have the right fit for both of you. As part of most agency's procedures, a thorough job description is formed and only candidates that are willing to do the entire list should be considered.

Take notes.

Interviewing requires superb listening skills, but listening isn't enough. Capture the details of the interview on paper to jog your memory, noting key actions and outcomes. Taking objective notes and recording responses will help you compare candidates when it's time to make a hiring decision.

One of the experts we look to in the recruiting field is Lou Adler, Best-selling Author and creator of "performance based hiring." His unique and sometimes ground-breaking views inform our business and interviewing practices at the agency. He relates to the interview process as a product sales scenario and suggests the following interview tips. Follow the links to learn more from his articles and books if you wish to go deeper into the interviewing topic.

The Discovery Process for the Interviewer

Step 1: Be different. Don't ask behavioral questions since all candidates have practiced answering these.

Step 2: Figure out what you're selling. Start by making sure everyone on the hiring team is familiar with the performance-based job description listing the top 4-5 performance objectives required for on-the-job success. Interviewing accuracy is dramatically improved when everyone knows what they're evaluating.

Step 3: Early in the interview find out why the candidate is looking for another job, most likely it's something involving economic need or lack of sufficient career growth. You'll use the balance of the interview to determine if your position meets these needs. This will be essential for negotiating the offer, especially if the person is a passive candidate and/or has multiple opportunities.

Step 4: Validate what you're buying. Use The Most Important Interview Question of All Time and the associated fact-finding questions to find out if the candidate is competent and motivated to do the actual work required. This involves describing one of the performance objectives and then asking the candidate to describe a comparable accomplishment. You'll need to do this for the 3-4 most important performance objectives to make an accurate assessment. From this you'll be able to determine if the gap between what you're offering and what the candidate has done is a career move, a lateral transfer or something below or beyond the candidate's current abilities.

Step 5: Determine thinking skills. Rather than using brainteasers to figure out thinking and problem-solving ability, ask about a real problem the person in the role is likely to face. (This is the second half of the two-question Performance-based Interview.) The purpose is to get into a back-and-forth dialogue to determine if the candidate's approach to solving the problem is appropriate. Focus on the process of getting the answer, not the answer itself. Then Anchor the question by getting an example of what the person has done that's most comparable to the problem being discussed.

Step 6: If the candidate is someone you'd like to consider, describe the opportunity gap and present your job as a true career move. Then find out the candidate's interest in further discussion. Whether you're on the hiring or job-seeking side it's important to recognize that an interview is a sales call. While figuring out who's the buyer and seller is a function of supply and demand, meeting the performance objectives for the job is what's being bought and sold. Unfortunately, too many companies, job-seekers and interviewers lose sight of the core purpose of the interview. You won't, if you put yourself in the shoes of a top sales rep on a 100% commission plan, and are always fully prepared.

Lou Adler is the Amazon best-selling author of *Hire With Your Head* (Wiley, 2007) and the award-winning Nightingale-Conant audio program, *Talent Rules!* His latest book, *The Essential Guide for Hiring & Getting Hired*, was published on February 1, 2013. You can learn more about Lou Adler's Most Important Interview Question and the 2 Question Interview at www.louadlergroup.com.

Reference and Background Checks

Checking applicants´ references is one of the most important procedures in the hiring process. Many job seekers misrepresent their backgrounds and credentials; others simply leave out important information. And no matter how honest applicants are, you can still learn a great deal by talking to other people who know them well. If you are working with an agency, the references of candidates should either be checked already, or will be thoroughly checked as you show continued interest in the applicant. Many employers like to have the agency provide them with a summary of the references they checked, and also the contact information to speak with the reference themselves. This is a very good idea, because hearing the enthusiasm (or lack of it) in someone's voice can tell you a great deal more than what they are saying.

Checking references takes time, but it can save you a lot of headaches down the road. A negative reference could keep you from hiring someone who is woefully unqualified for a job or who has destructive tendencies that could endanger you or your family. A simple reference check could trigger warnings that keep you from hiring a bad seed. The best rule of thumb: Always check applicants´ references or make sure the agency has checked them before the job offer is finalized.

Checking References

Tell all applicants that you will check their references before you make any hiring decisions. Employers often hire applicants because of a sharp-looking resume or a "good feeling" from an interview. No matter how quickly you would like to get a position filled, always perform due diligence before you take the hiring plunge.

Ask each applicant to sign a release form permitting you to ask detailed questions of former employers and other references. As part of the application process, an agency should already have this on file so you will be covered. The form prevents the applicant from suing you or any former employers based on the information you learn during the reference checks. Without this permission, you may only be able to confirm employment dates, pay rate and position -- information that tells you little about a prospective employee´s character.

Mention to the reference that you have a release from the applicant for any information the employer may give. Many employers fear being sued for defamation if they say anything negative about a former employee and will give only a brief or standard comment about the candidate. Keep in mind that some states now consider employers´ comments to be "qualifiedly privileged." That means the employer cannot be held liable for the information he reveals unless he knows it to be false or reckless. If that is the case in your state (check with your lawyer), make sure the references know it. Beware - Some employers give positive references even to bad ex-employees because they are afraid of legal action or are tired of paying unemployment taxes on the applicant.

Verify basic information such as employment dates, job titles, salary and types of jobs performed. If one of the basic checks does not match the applicant´s resume or what you heard during an interview, you should go back to the candidate for an explanation. The way the answer is handled will tell a lot about the person's candor and integrity. It will also reveal how they deal with a bit of a crisis and how they are able to "think on their feet."

Avoid vague questions. Ask specific questions based on details in the applicant's resume. For example: How did the employee contribute to specific functions or duties? Did they go above and beyond the call of duty to please an employer? Did they need close instruction and a watchful eye to do their job well, or were they effective working alone?

Pay attention to neutral or negative comments from references. Lukewarm comments or half-hearted praise speak volumes. Ask the former employer if they would hire the person back, and if they would recommend them for the new position in question. If they hesitate or "beat around the bush," you might need to move on to the next applicant. The other similar consideration is the occasional vindictive employer who wants to hurt an employee for leaving their employment. I have had to challenge some of the statements made by employers, especially if they alluded to theft or other improper behavior on the job. If there is a specific incident mentioned we want to know if it was documented or recorded, and especially if there were any criminal charges filed. This is a serious conversation that will affect a person's employment future, so there is no room for generalized accusation. Be sure of what you are hearing to consider the severity of any negative revelations.

Use former supervisors or senior coworkers as references. An applicant might not want you to contact their current employer (who might not know about the job hunt), but there are always people who can provide a reference. You may also wish to make the final job offer contingent upon a reference from their current position, if available. Don't discount this. We recently worked with an employer who insisted on calling the past employers directly, without exception. This eliminated over 90% of the great candidates we could have lined up for them. Many principals will simply not take a call for a reference, or it is inappropriate for the employee to ask them to do so.

It is also a good idea to check with an accounting department or business manager to confirm past salary. You might ask for a letter or copy of recent pay stubs for verification.

Author's note: References have become a bit trickier in recent years. Like the earlier warnings about employment laws, many employers and organizations are reluctant to offer their opinions about former employees. In several instances you may only receive a basic employment verification with dates and position title. Sometimes a candidate will be bound to a very tight confidentiality agreement and not be able to discuss their past employment at all. In a case where one or more past positions can't be checked, it will be critical to weigh the other available references and supporting documentation. As an agent we usually know which candidates will have difficulty getting a direct reference from a particular employer. We present these issues to clients during the introduction phase of our search to avoid confusion later on in the verifications stage.

Background Checks

Most agencies check the following background reports:

-Social Security records (to confirm if the person is who they say they are)
-State-by-state driving records (DMV)
-Criminal records (There are various levels of depth to criminal files. Ask your agency or provider to explain what type of reporting is available.)
-Civil litigation cases (whether suing an employer or being sued by another party)

-Other checks that may be performed, usually for an additional fee or simply upon request are:
-Consumer Credit History (This report has restrictions on its use for employment. Check with an attorney or your employment agency for state guidelines.)
-Military Records
-Transcripts or Certificates of Degrees and Certifications
-Pay stubs or tax records for income verification

When Should You Do a Background Check?

You should always conduct background checks before the candidate begins working for you, never after. It is much easier not to hire people than it is to fire them once they start. In most cases, all of the background questions have been asked of the applicant, and any pertinent information has already been revealed. So if you want to hire a candidate, simply make the start of employment contingent upon the actual verification of the facts through a private investigation firm. Agencies should have reputable sources for these types of checks. Ask what will be included as part of their screening process and what might be available in addition.

Don't worry that performing a background check will delay the start date or become a drawn out process. Many background checks take less than 48 hours. You'll be glad you did your check if it turns out that your prospective Executive Assistant has a conviction for financial theft, or your Driver candidate has been arrested twice for reckless driving! Perform any level of investigation that makes you comfortable trusting the new employee with your family and property.

All applicants through our agency are asked to fill out preliminary background forms to disclose any issues we might find in our screening, so we already have a head start and overall expectation that nothing negative will be found in the actual report.

Is There Something More...?

A great mentor of mine recently brainstormed with us about the services we provide. (Hat tip to Rob) Our goal was creating an authentic message and approach to the needs of our client base. Ultimately he suggested that our future would lie in moving beyond the fundamentals of our staffing service. Can we staff your home with employees that meet your criteria? Of course we can. We can do that all day and night, as good as anyone in the business. Sometimes it is that simple, and we are happy to work with you through the process of finding the right employees for your service needs. But we're way more tuned in these days, and sensing that the next phase of the client relationship is at hand. We've seen so many incidents of success and failure in private service that have nothing to do with a process or talent. This new era calls for a greater depth, and a larger view from a trusted service partner. So we have to ask, "Is there something more?"

We invite you to think outside of the box with us. What else is there in the service flow that we need to address? Do we need to admit some things, suggest some new things, or simply discard some things? What are we really talking about when we talk about service? How can we turn service from a trap into a freedom? Can we find peace in the seeming chaos of wealth and ownership? Can we return to gracefully receiving service, perhaps with a modern day edge? What is your new vision? How can we help?

The landscape has changed, and the new tools of luxury are at hand. Secrets are short lived and trust is the greatest of all luxuries. Do you have the roadmap to live out your vision successfully? Is your innermost circle secure and committed to your goals? How are you being represented to the world outside your immediate home and business environments? Do you feel protected in every sense of the word? Do you feel understood? Who is truly on your side?

We invite you to an agenda-free discussion. We're open to your ideas and a cooperative shaping of our business for everyone's benefit. As it is often said, "Help us help you." Let's explore the options and see where you are trying to go. We just might be able to guide you on the path.

Conclusion

Though the field of private service is a very specialized and unique place, many elements of success can be found in general, sound business advice. First and foremost, communication is essential for everyone involved from candidate to agent to employer. Make sure there are no hidden agendas and be honest with yourself as much as the person you may be entering into a long-term relationship with. Be as clear and open as possible every step of the way. The hiring and job hunting processes will eventually determine the path of someone's career and lifestyle. Usually it is both, and it applies to employers and employees alike. There is no way to be too prepared, or to do too much work, or have too much knowledge on the subject. The more one knows and understands about all of the contributing factors to their decisions, the better the decision will be in the long run. Don't take shortcuts and spare no reasonable expense along the path to finding the best scenario for all parties.

The concept of service in an employment context requires honest reflection and understanding. There is no perfect scenario or relationship, just a variety of ways to approach and imitate the ideal in any given service role. True service comes from the heart alone, with its ultimate practice seen in one person's unmerited sacrifice for another. Like a mother to a child, the greatest service model is in giving up one's own needs for the sake of another's comfort. We cannot obtain this level of giving in the employment context, but we can hold it up as the standard in theory. Within the business of private service we simply agree to play these roles for an agreed compensation, during a set period of time, which creates a fictional environment of servitude. Of course we can still care deeply about one another in the relationship, but we should recognize objectively that we are performing, and there is always compromise from both sides. Therefore it should be our goal as service providers to "act" in ways that emulate the ideal service relationship at all times. This is not always easy, but if you do naturally have a "service heart" you can come close to the pure act of self-giving service. And in doing so you can most certainly find contentment and joy in your work! For employers receiving service it is helpful to realize that no one is working for you out of obligation or pure sentiment, even if they have true talent and desire in serving. There is always a balance in what may be asked of a service provider and what can be offered in return. Our mutual goal in the business is to find a healthy flow in the structure of private service.

I have also found in my experience that there is a state of "knowing" where intuition seems to take over the screening and matching process. Things seem to "flow" better with a particular candidate or employer, or out of nowhere the perfect applicant for a job appears the day a client calls with an open position. These are usually the best placements and once the match is made it seems like it was obvious from day one that it would work. Though I would never substitute a feeling for sound, diligent screening techniques, I always pay attention to the subconscious factors in addition. I recommend this to all of the clients I deal with, especially at the in-person interview stages. Many times a deal is done because "It just feels right."

Lastly, enjoy yourself and accept whatever happens on your path as a learning experience. Not every situation will be perfect, no matter how hard everyone tries. If you reach the end of your rope and no comfortable solution is apparent, don't take it personally. Simply make a decision to move forward and try to exit the situation with the least amount of conflict. Overall, if you do your best to make a work environment healthy and productive for everyone, there will always be more winners than losers in private service.

About the Author

David Gonzalez is the Owner of Domestic Placement Network, an exclusive private staffing agency, and EstateJobs.com, the #1 site for private service job listings. He is a former Personal Assistant and House Manager to an entertainer where he interacted with ultra high net worth clients as both a guest and as an employee behind the scenes. This valuable insight led to a successful career on the agency side of the equation, helping top clients find and hire staff and assisting thousands of service professionals in their careers. He has been a featured speaker at industry events and is quoted in several major publications. He lives in Ojai, CA with his wife Lea and their two daughters Taylor and Alexandra.

Ways to connect:
Domestic Placement Network - Agency site: http://dpnonline.com
EstateJobs Job Site: http://estatejobs.com
Domestic Employment News and behind-the-scenes:
   http://domesticblog.com
LinkedIn discussion group for EstateJobs:
   http://www.linkedin.com/e/gis/807117
Facebook for job listings and industry updates:
   https://facebook.com/estatejobs
Twitter for job listings and news links: http://twitter.com/estatejobs

Call or email for additional resources or to discuss your private service needs.
Domestic Placement Network, LLC
PO Box 1326
Ojai, CA 93024
805-640-3608
Email: david@dpnonline.com

Made in the USA
Lexington, KY
25 January 2015